GW00373025

Road Accident Statistics
English Regions 1990

January 1992

London: HMSO

ISBN 0 11 551094 X

Prepared for publication by STD5 branch
Directorate of Statistics
Department of Transport

Richard Ackroyd
Andrew Colski
Yuk-Shu Ho

GOVERNMENT STATISTICAL SERVICE

A service of statistical information and advice is provided to the government by specialist staff employed in the statistics divisions of individual Departments. Statistics are made generally available through their publications and furtherinformation and advice on them can be obtained from the Departments concerned.

Enquiries about the contents of this publication should be made to:

Directorate of Statistics
Department of Transport
Room B6.48
Romney House
43 Marsham Street
London SW1P 3PY

Telephone 071 276 8785

Data Service

Copies of the main tables in this publication can be supplied on a computer diskette by the Department of Transport (at a cost of £40). Further tabulations of road accident statistics are also available from the Department, subject to confidentiality rules. The charges vary with the complexity of the analysis (minimum £40) and the availability of these services depends upon the resources within the Department. Enquiries should be addressed in writing to Mr A L Colski at the above address

Produced from camera ready copy supplied by the department. The price of this publication has been set to make some contribution to the preparation costs incurred at the Department of Transport

Printed in the United Kingdom for HMSO.
Dd.295499, 1/92, C8, 3390/3, 5673, 182377.

CONTENTS   **Page**

Symbols and Conventions

Rounding of Figures

In tables where figures have been rounded there may be an apparent slight discrepancy between the sum of the constituent items and the independently rounded total.

Symbols

The following symbols have been used throughout:

'-' = nil or negligible (less than half the final digit shown)

'..' = not available

Conversion Factor

1 kilometre = 0.6214 mile

INTRODUCTION

This is the tenth edition of Road Accident Statistics English Regions (RASER), a Government Statistical Service publication which gives statistics of road accidents on a local basis for England. RASER concentrates on accidents as being incidents which may reflect a need for local action and is intended to be of most benefit to traffic engineers, planners and administrators in local government and the Department of Transport (DTp) regional offices. For this reason, most of the data in the book are compiled according to the county groupings covered by these offices (which are shown on the map on the adjoining page).

RASER is confined to background national statistics, so it should be regarded as a supplement to 'Road Accidents Great Britain 1990 - The Casualty Report' (RAGB), which is the main publication on road accident statistics in Great Britain. RAGB is available from HMSO bookshops, price £9.95.

The current system of collecting road accident statistics was set up in 1968, and is for the benefit and use of local authorities, the police and central government. Each year, about 250,000 STATS19 road accident report forms (an example of which can be found on pages 42 to 44) are completed by police officers of the 51 police forces in Great Britain. These forms record data about accidents on the public highway which involved personal injury or death. These data are transferred onto magnetic tape and are sent to the DTp where they are incorporated into an annual data file.

The principal purpose in collecting and publishing statistics of road accidents is to provide background information for both central government and local authorities on the roads, road users, places, times of day, weather conditions, where road accidents happen etc, and against which various remedial measures can be considered. Road accident statistics are used to provide both a local and a national perspective for particular road safety problems or particular suggested remedies. A continuous flow of information - such as the time series tables in this book - means that trends of accidents and casualties can be examined and used to change the direction of policies when necessary.

The format of this edition of RASER is broadly similar to that of last year. The report also includes data from Northern Ireland. These data, where available, are included with each table along with data for Scotland and Wales. *More detailed statistics for Scotland and Wales are available from the Scottish and Welsh Offices - please refer to the inside rear cover for more details.*

Several of the tables contain averages of 1981-85 data. These represent the base figures which the Secretary of State for Transport used to set the target of reducing the number of road casualties by one third by the year 2000. It should also be noted that main Tables 1 and 6 which give casualty totals by severity for the years covering 1981 to 1985 have been extended to show revised estimates for London for this period. At the beginning of September 1984 the Metropolitan police implemented improved procedures for allocating the level of severity to accidents and casualties. The change is thought to have had no effect on overall casualty numbers, but in the period between 1981 and the date of the change it is estimated that there were 4,725 casualties whose injuries were originally judged to be slight but would have been judged serious under the later procedures. However, this is an overall estimate and it is not possible to present similar revised estimates of accidents by road type and other detailed characteristics.

The Department of Transport is generally prepared to sell tabulations of road accident data. The cost of data varies with the complexity of each request, but averages about £40 per year of data. Further information can be obtained from: - *Andrew Colski, Department of Transport, Room B648, Romney House, 43 Marsham Street, London SW1P 3PY, Telephone 071-276-8785.*

DEPARTMENT OF TRANSPORT REGIONAL ORGANISATION

AS AT MAY 1991

Location of Regional Offices ● LEEDS

NORTHERN
Wellbar House
Gallowgate
Newcastle upon Tyne
NE1 4TU

☎ 091 2327575
(GTN 5227)

YORKSHIRE AND HUMBERSIDE
City House
New Station Street
Leeds
LS1 4JD

☎ 0532 438232
(GTN 5173)

NORTH WEST
Sunley Tower
Piccadilly Plaza
Manchester
M1 4BE

☎ 061 832 9111
(GTN 4301)

Note
GTN (Government Telephone Network) numbers are not available on the public telephone system.

WEST MIDLANDS
Five Ways Tower
Frederick Road
Edgbaston
Birmingham
B15 1SJ

☎ 021 631 4141
(GTN 6161)

No 5 Broadway
Broad Street
Birmingham
B15 1BL

☎ 021 631 8000
(GTN 2973)

EAST MIDLANDS
Cranbrook House
Cranbrook street
Nottingham
NG1 1EY

☎ 0602 476121
(GTN 6202)

EASTERN
49–51 Heron House
Goldington Road
Bedford
MK40 3LL

☎ 0234 363161
(GTN 3013)

SOUTH WEST
Tollgate House
Houlton Street
Bristol
BS2 9DJ

☎ 0272 218811
(GTN 1374)

Sub office:—
Falcon Road
Sowton
Exeter
EX2 7LB

☎ 0392 216609
(GTN 1365)

SOUTH EAST
Federated House
London Road
Dorking
Surrey
RH4 1SZ

☎ 0306 885922
(GTN 3624)

Senet House
Station Road
Dorking
Surrey
RH4 1H5

☎ 0306 742025
(GTN 2904)

LONDON REGIONAL OFFICE
2 Marsham Street
London
SW1P 3EB

☎ 071 276 3000
(GTN 276)

Further copies of this map may be obtained from:
HGU Drawing Office
P2/019, 2 Marsham St.

Department of Transport
HGU Drawing Office 91 044

1. Commentary on main tables

Richard Ackroyd

Foreword

This section gives a review of the main body of tables included in this report. As noted in the introduction, the data in most of the tables are disaggregated either by county or DTp region and Northern Ireland data have been included within certain tables. Tables where Northern Ireland data are not available, and thus where no United Kingdom total can be given, have been individually annotated.

1.1. Casualties

Table 1 gives the regional distribution of casualties and is presented as a time series for the period 1984 to 1990. The average for the years 1981-1985 is also given. There has been little significant change in casualty distribution over this period. In each of the seven years shown, London has had the largest number of casualties. In the years 1984 to 1989 the next highest number of casualties was found in the South East region but in 1990 the North West region had the next highest. The lowest number of casualties was in the Northern region, which consistently has half those of the East Midland region, the next lowest in England.

In 1990, as in 1989, London also had the highest casualty rate per 100,000 population, followed by the Eastern and North West regions. The lowest rates were found in the Northern and South West regions. London, however, had the lowest fatality rate of all the regions - probably because accidents in urban areas tend to be less severe because they occur at lower speeds. The highest fatality rate was found in the East Midlands region with the next highest in the Eastern region.

1.2. Local authority casualty comparisons

Tables 2-5 give information on the number of casualties, rate per 100,000 population, and percentage distribution, by age and road user type for each English county.

Table 2 gives the number of casualties by age and road user type for 1990 and **Table 3** gives the same information as an average for the years 1981-1985.

Table 4 gives casualty rates, per 100,000 population, by age and by type of road user for each English county. In England in 1990, 415 children were injured in road accidents per 100,000 children and the county casualty rates varied from 242 in Avon to 576 in Greater Manchester. The casualty rate for those aged 60 and over varied from 173 in the Isle of Wight to 457 in Nottinghamshire. The overall casualty rate for all ages was lowest in Avon and highest in Surrey. The pedestrian casualty rate was highest in most urbanised counties, in particular, London, Greater Manchester, and Merseyside and lowest in rural counties such as Suffolk and Somerset. The pedal cyclist casualty rate was highest in Cambridgeshire and lowest in Durham and Northumberland. The car occupant casualty rate varied from 191 in Avon to 516 in Surrey.

Table 5 gives the distribution of casualties, by age and by type of road user, for each county. In England in 1990, 13 per cent of road accident casualties were children and 11 per cent were aged 60 and over. The proportion of casualties who were children varied from 9 per cent in Gloucestershire to 18 per cent in Tyne & Wear. East Sussex had the highest proportion of elderly casualties; 16 per cent compared with 11 per cent in the whole of England.

Table 6 gives the number of fatal and serious casualties and total casualties for each English county for 1990 and compares them with the average for the years 1981-1985. The percentage change is also given. In England, fatal and serious casualties fell by 17 per cent but the total number of casualties rose by 6 per cent. The number of casualties killed and seriously injured fell in every county except Cambridgeshire, Cheshire, and Northumberland.

Table 7 gives the total number of casualties in each region disaggregated by severity and by road type. In all regions, over 50 per cent of casualties were in accidents on built-up roads, and no more than 5 per cent in motorway accidents. The proportion of those casualties killed and seriously injured was highest on non-built up roads.

Table 8 gives the casualty rates by severity for motorways and A roads for each region. The casualty rate is derived by dividing the number of casualties on a particular road type by the traffic carried on those roads. The rates are given as an average over the period 1988 to 1990. The data show that the highest 'all severities' rate on motorways was found in London, with the lowest in the West Midlands region. London also had the highest 'all severities' rate for all A roads, and the South West the lowest rate. For England as a whole, the highest 'all severities' rate is found on built-up trunk and principal roads, and the lowest on motorways.

1.3. Injury accident rates

Table 9 gives the rates for accidents involving personal injury for motorways and A roads. The accident rate is derived by dividing the number of accidents on roads of a particular type by the traffic carried on that type of road. The rates are given as an average over the period 1988 to 1990. The data show that, in England over the three year period, built-up principal A roads had the highest accident rate at 112 accidents per 100 million vehicle kilometres and motorways the lowest rate at 11 accidents per 100 million vehicle kilometres. The table also shows that accident rates were generally higher on principal A roads than on trunk A roads.

1.4. Seasonal patterns

The seasonal pattern of injury accidents is given in **Table 10**. The peak months for accidents can vary from year to year for various reasons, for example, differing weather conditions.

The general pattern is low accident numbers in the early part of the year, gradually building up to a peak in May, June and July, followed by a small dip and then a higher peak in October and November. This trend continued in 1990, with the peak month for accidents falling in either October or November for all regions except the South West. When accident figures are related to the number of days in each month, March contains the fewest number of accidents per day in six of the English regions with December having the fewest in the remaining three regions. November has the highest number of accidents per day in all but one region. The pattern for fatal and serious accidents generally follows that for all accidents, with the peak month for these accidents, in number and by day, varying between January and November in most regions.

1.5. Injury accidents by type of road, county, and region

Tables 11-13 show the number of junction and non-junction injury accidents occurring on motorways and trunk and principal A roads. On motorways in England, 15 per cent of accidents occurred at junctions and roundabouts. On trunk A roads, 56 per cent of accidents occurred at junctions and roundabouts as did 68 per cent of accidents on principal A roads.

Junction accidents, including those on roundabouts, account for about 50 per cent of all trunk A road accidents in each region except London, where the proportion of junction accidents rises to almost 70 per cent. The proportion of motorway junction accidents was much lower ranging from 9 per cent in the South West and West Midlands regions to 29 per cent in the London region.

Table 14 gives the total number of injury accidents disaggregated by severity on different types of road in each region and county for 1989 and 1990. The average for the years 1981 to 1985 is also given. The road classifications used are motorways, trunk and principal A roads and all roads.

Table 15 shows injury accidents and casualties by severity, and the vehicles involved, for individual English motorways, including A(M) roads. 80 per cent of the vehicles involved were cars or vans while 15 per cent were heavy lorries, broadly in line with their share of motorway traffic. Motorways with the highest numbers of accidents per kilometre in 1990 were the M25 (4.3 accidents), the M63 (3.8 accidents), and the M4 (3.6 accidents).

Table 16 gives the percentage of accidents on the various types of road within each region. This table should be considered in conjunction with Table 19 which shows the distribution of motor traffic within each region.

1.6. Background data

Table 17 gives regional background information on road lengths, home population, area, and licensed vehicle numbers. Table 18 gives the 1988-1990 average distribution between regions of motor traffic on major roads, and Table 19 shows the distribution of motor traffic within each region. The English motorway lengths shown in Tables 15 and 17 have been supplied by DTp Highways Computing Division from data extracted from the Network Information System (NIS). Other road lengths in Table 17 are taken from the Transport Statistics Report 'Road Lengths in Great Britain 1990'.

APPENDIX

This appendix lists the table numbers in this report and compares them with the equivalent table numbers for the previous four editions of RASER.

Year of report

1990	1989	1988	1987	1986

Table number

1990	1989	1988	1987	1986
1	1	1	1	1
2	2	-	-	-
3	3	-	-	-
4	4	2	2	-
5	5	3	3	-
6	6	4	4	-
7	7	-	-	-
8	8	-	-	-
9	9	5	5	2
10	10	6	6	3
11	11	7	7	4a
12	12	8a	8	4b
13	13	8b	-	-
14	14	9	9	5a
15	16	10	10	-
16	15	11	11	6
17	17	12	12	7
18	18	13	13	8a
19	19	14	14	8b

2. Injury accidents and casualties on the M25 from 1987 to 1990

Andrew Colski

2.1. Introduction

In October 1986, eleven years after the first section was opened, the M25 London Orbital Motorway was completed. This article examines the record of injury accidents on the M25 in the first four calendar years of the operation of the whole road, 1987 to 1990. Comparison is made between the M25 and other motorways, and between individual sections of the M25.

The injury accident record of the M25 in previous years was examined in articles published in 'Road Accident Statistics English Regions', 1985 and 1986. These were brief summaries of the number and rate of accidents on those sections of the motorway which were open in these years. In both years the rate of injury accidents on the M25 per hundred million vehicle kilometres was comparable with that for all motorways in England. The rate for fatal and serious accidents was lower than average on the M25.

Almost all of the London Orbital Motorway is classified as the M25, though the section from Junction 31 at Thurrock to Junction 2 at Dartford, including the Dartford Tunnel, is classified as the A282. When looking at accidents on each section of the M25 this article also considers those sections which form the A282. When comparing the M25 with other motorways the A282 sections have not been included, so that comparisons are made only between roads of motorway standard. The new Queen Elizabeth II bridge between Dartford and Thurrock, which forms part of the A282 link, was opened in the autumn of 1991. During the period considered by this article the tunnel alone was in operation.

2.2. History of injury accidents and casualties on the M25

Table 2a shows the number of accidents and casualties on the M25, A282 and on all motorways in Great Britain, over the period 1987 to 1990. It also shows the growth in traffic and road length. During these years the M25 accounted for 12 per cent of all motorway injury accidents and casualties, but only 10 per cent of fatal or serious casualties. The total number of injury accidents on the M25 increased by 19 per cent between 1987 and 1990, compared to an increase of 21 per cent on all motorways. There were similar increases in the number of casualties on the M25 and on all motorways. These increases in injury accidents and casualties closely reflect the growth in traffic both on the M25 and on all motorways.

Table 2a: Injury accidents and casualties on the M25 and all motorways: GB 1987 to 1990

	Accidents				Casualties				Indices (1987=100)	
	Fatal	Serious	Slight	Total	Fatal	Serious	Slight	Total	Traffic	Length
M25:										
1987	13	115	557	685	21	145	879	1,045	100	100
1988	22	107	576	705	29	139	883	1,051	109	100
1989	15	126	648	789	19	158	1,026	1,203	115	100
1990	19	136	658	813	25	182	1,036	1,243	119	100
A282:										
1987	1	6	28	35	1	6	44	51	100	100
1988	1	5	36	42	1	6	56	63	108	100
1989	0	6	39	45	0	7	58	65	115	100
1990	0	5	42	47	0	5	64	69	114	100
All Motorways[1]										
1987	212	1,137	4,177	5,526	283	1,583	7,214	9,080	100	100
1988	216	1,069	4,363	5,648	242	1,448	7,083	8,773	109	101
1989	193	1,142	5,074	6,409	233	1,583	8,326	10,142	119	101
1990	183	1,171	5,352	6,706	229	1,651	8,989	10,869	122	103

1 Includes M and A(M) roads.

The number of people killed or seriously injured (KSI) in accidents on the M25 increased by 25 per cent, from 166 in 1987 to 207 in 1990. This compares with an overall increase of just 1 per cent in the number killed or seriously injured on all motorways. Most of the 25 per cent increase on the M25 occurred between 1989 and 1990, when the number of casualties KSI on the M25 increased by 17 per cent, compared with a 3.5 per cent increase on all motorways over the same period. Traffic growth was smallest between these two years.

2.3. Injury accident record of each section of the M25 and A282

Table 2b shows the number of injury accidents on each section of the M25 and A282, in each of the years from 1987 to 1990. It also gives comparative accident rates in terms of traffic and road length, as an average over all four years. Given the relatively small numbers of injury accidents on each individual section, apparently large fluctuations between years are not necessarily significant or indicative of conditions on any single section.

Table 2b: Injury accidents and accident rates on the M25 and A282: Individual sections: 1987 to 1990

| Section (junction) | Length (Km) | Number of Accidents | | | | Annual Average 1987-90 | Accident rates (1987-1990 averages) | |
		1987	1988	1989	1990		Annual rate per 100 million vehicle kilometres	Annual rate per kilometre of road
A282:								
31-1a	3.5	15	26	19	27	22	21.2	6.2
1a-1b	2.3	15	9	13	16	13	19.1	5.8
1b-2	1.3	5	4	9	4	6	13.1	4.2
M25:								
2-3	5.3	11	5	22	22	15	9.7	2.8
3-4	5.6	8	8	5	10	8	6.1	1.4
4-5	6.6	5	10	16	11	11	6.5	1.6
5-6	15.4	41	38	43	50	43	8.8	2.8
6-7	4.6	19	14	17	21	18	11.2	3.9
7-8	5.3	18	26	21	24	22	10.8	4.2
8-9	10.6	58	46	39	50	48	12.9	4.6
9-10	9.0	41	37	61	39	45	14.0	4.9
10-11	7.7	41	40	46	43	43	12.5	5.5
11-12	3.5	26	31	14	10	20	13.1	5.8
12-13	5.1	40	31	34	25	33	12.8	6.4
13-14	3.1	12	30	31	43	29	17.2	9.4
14-15	3.2	13	11	17	15	14	8.6	4.4
15-16	8.4	38	47	40	38	41	10.1	4.9
16-17	8.8	41	38	53	40	43	11.4	4.9
17-18	2.3	13	8	9	3	8	8.2	3.6
18-19	4.1	23	22	22	18	21	11.1	5.2
19-20	2.8	5	4	13	15	9	8.6	3.3
20-21	4.7	21	15	27	27	23	11.9	4.8
21-21a	1.0	0	1	4	6	3	..	2.8
21a-22	6.9	15	14	19	13	15	6.4	2.2
22-23	4.8	6	6	15	6	8	4.4	1.7
23-24	4.3	20	34	33	37	31	19.4	7.2
24-25	8.8	23	49	23	38	33	10.5	3.8
25-26	5.8	12	16	11	20	15	7.5	2.5
26-27	6.9	36	42	38	51	42	13.8	6.1
27-28	12.6	46	43	49	46	46	9.8	3.7
28-29	4.3	8	8	13	8	9	7.0	2.2
29-30	8.7	23	26	46	34	32	13.9	3.7
30-31	1.6	5	10	7	10	8	19.4	5.0
Total[1]	195.3	703	749	829	820[2]	797[2]	11.2	4.1

1 Combined total for A282 and M25. Excludes accidents on link and spur roads at junctions 4, 9, 19 and 31.
2 Excludes 18 accidents in 1990 which had not been allocated to individual sections at the time of publication.

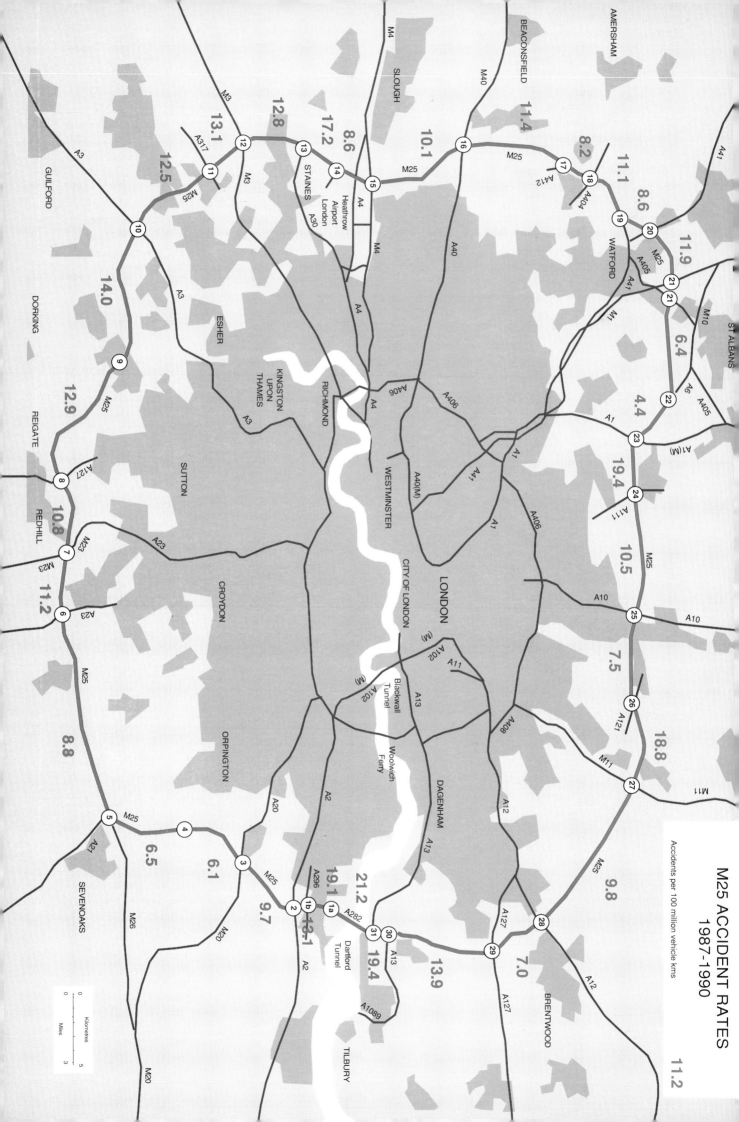

M25 ACCIDENT RATES
1987-1990

Accidents per 100 million vehicle kms

Accident, traffic and road length data in **Table 2b** are derived from the Department of Transport's Network Information System (NIS), which is operated by the Highways Computing Division. Accident data in NIS is taken from the national injury accident reporting system, which is based on STATS19 forms completed by the police, a copy of which can be found on pages 40-42 of this report. NIS allocates accidents to particular trunk roads and links, using a range of data from the STATS19 form, whereas data in other tables use only the recorded first road class, taken directly from STATS19 reports. Thus there is a slight difference between the accident totals in table 2b and data in other tables. There are no traffic data for the short section between Junctions 21 and 21a, the M1 and A405 interchanges.

Throughout the period from 1987 to 1990 the highest number of accidents have occurred on the Sevenoaks to Godstone section (Junctions 5-6), the Reigate to Chertsey section (Junctions 8 to 11), the M4 to Maple Cross section (Junctions 15 to 17), and the Waltham Abbey to Brentwood section (Junctions 26 to 28). These include the longest individual sections of the motorway. However, the sections with the highest traffic flows, between the M3 at Thorpe and the M40 at Denham (Junctions 12 to 16), did not have a correspondingly large number of accidents. This may be because on these busier sections traffic is slower and injury accidents less likely to occur.

Accident rates per 100 million vehicle kilometres for each section are shown on the map of the M25 on the opposite page. These rates give a comparison between sections which takes into account varying levels of traffic. The highest rate is found on the Dartford Tunnel section, Junctions 31 to 1a, with an average rate of 21.2 over the four years. The sections on either side of the Tunnel also have high rates (Junctions 30 to 31 and 1a to 1b). Only the section between the A1(M) at South Mimms and Potters Bar (Junctions 23 to 24) has a comparable accident rate, at 19.4, while the Waltham Abbey to Theydon Bois M11 section (Junctions 26 to 27) and the Egham to Poyle section (Junctions 13 to 14), have slightly lower rates, at 18.8 and 17.2 respectively.

The lowest rates per 100 million vehicle kilometres are found on the section between the M1 and A1(M), Junctions 21a to 23, and the Swanley to Sevenoaks section, Junctions 3 to 5, all between 4.4 and 6.5. The Brentwood to Upminster section (Junctions 28 to 29) and the Bull's Cross to Waltham Abbey section (Junctions 25 to 26) have slightly higher rates, at 7.0 and 7.5 respectively.

Rates per kilometre of road are broadly in line with rates in terms of traffic. The highest is on the Egham to Poyle section (Junctions 13 to 14), which has a rate of 9.4 accidents per kilometre per year, and the lowest rate of 1.4 is found on the Swanley to Shoreham section (Junctions 3 to 4). Sections which have relatively higher rates in terms of road length than in terms of traffic are among the busier sections and include the Thorpe to Egham section (Junctions 12 to 13), the Rickmansworth to Watford section (Junctions 18 to 19) and the Poyle to Denham section (Junctions 14 to 16). The Upminster to Thurrock section (Junctions 29 to 31) has relatively lower rates per kilometre of road than per 100 million vehicle kilometres.

2.4. Comparisons with other motorways

Table 2c shows the number of injury accidents and casualties on the M25 and other major motorways in Great Britain, in each of the years 1987 to 1990. More accidents have occurred on the M1, M4 and M6 than on the M25 in each of these years. Together these four roads account for 55 per cent of all motorway injury accidents in Great Britain, while carrying 48 per cent of motorway traffic and covering 37 per cent of motorway length.

Table 2d gives comparative accident and casualty rates for the same motorways, averaged over the period 1987 to 1990. In terms of road length the M25 has the highest accident rate for any motorway, with 3.97 accidents per kilometre of road. Only the M1, with a rate of 3.20, and the M4, with a rate of 2.77, have a rate approaching that of the M25. The rate of casualties killed or seriously injured (KSI) per kilometre of road is 0.95 on the M25. This is only exceeded by a rate of 1.01 on the M1 and 0.99 on the M3.

13

Table 2c: Injury accidents and casualties: By selected motorways: GB: 1987-1990

Road	Casualties								Accidents			
	1987		1988		1989		1990		1987	1988	1989	1990
	KSI	All	KSI	All	KSI	All	KSI	All				
M25[1]	166	1,045	168	1,051	177	1,203	207	1,243	685	705	789	813
M1	341	1,613	266	1,510	336	1,646	281	1,674	914	955	968	1,021
M2	41	125	44	136	15	146	16	125	77	69	100	70
M3	60	264	106	284	83	317	86	335	170	186	185	206
M4	233	1,176	239	1,161	236	1,292	265	1,452	691	763	835	888
M5	144	535	122	549	119	560	132	642	310	313	338	371
M6	283	1,422	185	1,252	247	1,539	296	1,654	767	753	929	932
M8	43	229	65	221	49	307	57	339	150	150	203	188
M9	3	23	6	25	16	49	10	53	19	20	32	34
M11	60	224	36	182	33	247	25	216	147	116	163	134
M18	10	53	14	73	15	67	13	51	35	35	39	34
M20	25	102	13	60	18	81	17	110	70	43	57	64
M27	32	128	23	111	38	164	34	154	88	83	109	112
M40	20	119	19	102	22	117	19	138	69	66	79	100
M42	15	67	23	69	17	91	27	112	45	54	68	74
M50	5	13	5	12	7	19	10	56	8	10	12	17
M56	19	138	13	101	27	141	22	158	95	81	95	101
M61	32	87	10	52	17	115	9	104	46	35	65	73
M62	73	488	84	533	89	555	99	616	319	351	367	398
M90	13	42	24	67	15	52	7	30	29	38	29	22
M180	11	24	2	16	2	12	8	29	15	10	9	18
All M'ways[2]	1,866	9,080	1,690	8,773	1,816	10,142	1,880	10,869	5,526	5,648	6,409	6,706

1 Excludes A282.
2 Includes other motorways and A(M) roads. Excludes A282.

Taking account of traffic levels, the rate of accidents on the M25 is slightly above average, at 11.65 per 100 million vehicle kilometres. The highest rate of 17.10 is found on the M8. The M1, M2, M3, M4 and M27 also have higher accident rates than the M25. The rate of casualties KSI per 100 million vehicle kilometres is below average on the M25, at 2.80. The M3 and M8 have the highest rates, at 5.39 and 5.30 respectively. The M56 and M40 have the lowest rates, at 2.10 and 2.18 respectively.

Table 2d also shows the average daily flow on each motorway. The M25 is by far the busiest motorway, having an average traffic flow of 93.5 thousand vehicles per kilometre per day, nearly twice the average of 50.2 thousand on all motorways. No other motorway has such a high average traffic flow. This is why the M25 has relatively high accident rates in terms of its length, but is closer to the average rates in terms of traffic.

The rate of casualties killed or seriously injured per accident gives an indication of the relative severity of accidents which occur on each motorway. The M25 has one of the lowest rates of casualties KSI per accident, at 0.24, which suggests that injury accidents on the M25 tend to be less severe than on other motorways. This is reflected in the M25 having relatively lower KSI rates than accident rates. The M62 has a similar rate to the M25, while only the M56 has a lower rate, at 0.22 casualties KSI per accident. The highest rate of 0.57 is found on the M50.

14.8 per cent of vehicles involved in injury accidents on the M25 between 1987 and 1990 were Heavy Goods Vehicles. This is close to the average of 14.9 per cent on all motorways, but is lower than most of the major motorways listed here, including the M1, M2, M5, M6 and M62. The highest involvement of HGVs in injury accidents is found on the M18 and M50, while the lowest is found on the M8 and M27. HGVs accounted for 15 per cent of traffic on the M25 and on all motorways between 1987 and 1990. The involvement of HGVs in injury accidents probably reflects levels of HGV traffic.

Road	Length (kms)[3]	Traffic (100 mil veh kms)[4]	Mean Flow (1000 vehs per day)[5]	Rates (1987-1990 average) KSI per km of road	Accidents per km of road	KSI per 100m veh kms	Accidents per 100 m veh kms	Number KSI per accident	Percentage (1987-1990 average) % of vehs involved were HGVs	% of accs in rain or snow	% of accs in fog
M25[1]	188	64.20	93.5	0.95	3.97	2.80	11.65	0.24	14.8%	12.7%	1.7%
M1	302	71.98	65.4	1.01	3.20	4.25	13.40	0.32	16.5%	15.7%	1.7%
M2	42	5.93	38.3	0.68	1.86	4.89	13.33	0.37	18.4%	17.7%	4.4%
M3	85	15.53	50.2	0.99	2.20	5.39	12.03	0.45	11.0%	15.7%	1.6%
M4	287	61.05	58.3	0.85	2.77	3.98	13.01	0.31	11.1%	18.7%	1.8%
M5	262	42.58	44.6	0.49	1.27	3.04	7.82	0.39	15.4%	15.9%	1.4%
M6	371	74.83	55.2	0.68	2.28	3.38	11.30	0.30	19.8%	21.5%	1.8%
M8	76	10.10	36.4	0.70	2.27	5.30	17.10	0.31	9.8%	25.5%	1.2%
M9	52	3.25	17.1	0.17	0.50	2.69	8.08	0.33	14.5%	22.9%	1.0%
M11	84	12.13	39.6	0.46	1.67	3.18	11.55	0.28	15.2%	15.2%	2.7%
M18	46	3.70	21.9	0.28	0.77	3.51	9.66	0.36	26.3%	14.0%	4.9%
M20	61	7.00	31.4	0.30	0.96	2.61	8.36	0.31	14.4%	17.9%	2.6%
M27	54	7.45	38.1	0.59	1.83	4.26	13.15	0.32	8.8%	16.3%	1.0%
M40	48	9.18	52.7	0.42	1.65	2.18	8.56	0.25	10.8%	14.6%	3.5%
M42	67	6.08	24.8	0.31	0.90	3.37	9.92	0.34	17.7%	15.4%	2.1%
M50	35	1.73	13.6	0.19	0.34	3.91	6.81	0.57	25.8%	6.4%	6.4%
M56	58	9.65	45.6	0.35	1.60	2.10	9.64	0.22	15.9%	21.2%	1.9%
M61	38	6.10	44.2	0.45	1.45	2.79	8.98	0.31	14.4%	25.6%	1.8%
M62	173	35.08	55.6	0.50	2.08	2.46	10.23	0.24	19.3%	25.3%	2.1%
M90	49	3.75	21.0	0.30	0.60	3.93	7.87	0.50	12.6%	16.9%	0.8%
M180	41	2.25	15.1	0.14	0.32	2.56	5.78	0.44	23.4%	19.2%	1.9%
All M/ways[2]	3,070	563.05	50.2	0.59	1.98	3.22	10.78	0.30	14.9%	18.0%	1.8%

1 Excludes A282.
2 Includes other motorways and A(M) roads. Excludes A282.
3 Length as at May 1990. Excluding slip roads.
4 100 million vehicle kilometres. 1987 to 1990 average.
5 Traffic (1987-90) / Road length (1990).

The M25 has one of the lowest proportions of injury accidents in rain or snow, at 12.7 per cent. The highest proportions are found on the M8, M9, M61 and M62. 1.7 per cent of accidents on the M25 occur in fog, slightly below average. The M50, M18 and M40 have the highest proportion of accidents in fog. This shows that the M25 has a relatively high proportion of fair weather accidents. These figures probably reflect local climatic conditions which affect each motorway.

2.5. Conclusion

Over the period 1987 to 1990 the number of injury accidents on the M25 increased by 19 per cent, compared to an increase of 21 per cent on all motorways. The M25 has only a slightly higher than average rate of accidents when volume of traffic is taken into account and, although the number of fatal and serious casualties has risen significantly since 1987, the rate of casualties KSI per 100 million vehicle kilometres remains below the average for all motorways. The rate of accidents per kilometre of road is higher on the M25 than on any other motorway and it has one of the highest rates of fatal or serious injuries per kilometre of road amongst all motorways. This reflects the heavy flow of traffic on the M25.

The M25 is one of the most important motorways in Great Britain, forming a major part of the Trunk road network and carrying 11 per cent of all motorway traffic between 1987 and 1990. In terms of the number of injury accidents and the volume of traffic it compares with other major motorways, such as the M1, M4 and M6. However, the flow of vehicles per kilometre of road is much greater than on any other motorway and accidents tend to be less severe. Thus whilst the M25 is clearly the busiest and most crowded motorway in the country, the level of injury accidents is comparable with other major motorways carrying similar volumes of traffic.

LIST OF TABLES AND CHARTS

1 Casualties: by region and severity: 1981-5 average, 1984-1990: rate per 100,000 population, 1990

Number/rate

	1981-5 Average	1984	1985	1986	1987	1988	1989	1990	1990 Rate Per 100,000 Population
Northern									
Killed	221	218	185	209	222	213	210	246	9.5
Killed or seriously injured	2,637	2,591	2,425	2,417	2,228	2,260	2,248	2,271	87.9
All Casualties	11,107	10,858	10,860	10,989	11,078	11,208	12,741	13,001	503.3
Yorkshire and Humberside									
Killed	501	495	450	499	440	437	480	428	8.6
Killed or seriously injured	6,830	6,745	6,259	6,559	5,817	6,131	6,127	5,978	120.7
All Casualties	25,915	25,525	25,255	25,922	25,328	26,884	28,560	28,455	574.6
East Midlands									
Killed	492	489	466	458	448	413	514	513	12.8
Killed or seriously injured	6,389	6,300	5,546	5,516	5,254	5,031	5,342	5,045	125.5
All Casualties	23,079	22,957	22,584	22,819	22,494	23,308	25,129	24,852	618.4
Eastern									
Killed	601	601	571	606	614	587	617	608	10.6
Killed or seriously injured	9,312	9,237	8,935	8,734	8,318	8,230	7,967	7,653	132.9
All Casualties	33,789	35,228	34,682	36,527	35,886	37,896	39,424	37,908	658.3
South East									
Killed	735	768	664	698	676	718	715	699	10.0
Killed or seriously injured	11,038	11,006	10,629	10,134	9,446	9,321	8,766	8,155	117.1
All Casualties	41,999	43,745	41,874	41,920	40,326	41,184	43,050	42,387	608.6
London[1]									
Killed	539	571	493	520	456	446	460	408	6.0
Killed or seriously injured	8,230	8,001	9,558	8,798	9,517	9,478	9,344	8,910	131.1
	(9,175)	(8,841)							
All Casualties	54,156	53,871	51,469	51,610	49,454	50,114	52,779	51,871	763.4
South West									
Killed	484	485	463	459	457	462	521	468	10.0
Killed or seriously injured	8,047	7,863	7,183	7,305	6,250	6,134	5,781	5,424	116.2
All Casualties	26,352	26,677	25,936	26,178	24,507	25,444	25,246	25,034	536.5
West Midlands									
Killed	526	522	491	506	442	442	498	478	9.2
Killed or seriously injured	7,857	8,001	7,210	6,853	5,860	5,774	6,190	6,136	117.6
All Casualties	27,699	28,122	27,339	27,409	25,425	26,760	28,964	30,219	579.0
North West									
Killed	600	605	539	591	594	565	572	575	8.4
Killed or seriously injured	7,049	6,890	6,478	6,318	6,079	5,859	6,048	6,249	90.8
All Casualties	36,286	37,032	36,510	37,521	37,963	39,196	42,059	43,749	635.8
England									
Killed	4,698	4,754	4,322	4,546	4,349	4,283	4,587	4,423	9.2
Killed or seriously injured	67,388	66,634	64,223	62,634	58,769	58,218	57,813	55,821	116.7
All Casualties	280,382	284,015	276,509	280,895	272,461	281,994	297,952	297,476	621.8
Wales									
Killed	259	246	242	235	220	226	233	249	8.6
Killed or seriously injured	3,855	3,698	3,548	3,478	3,388	3,127	3,191	3,037	105.4
All Casualties	14,395	14,141	13,767	14,446	14,266	15,164	16,165	16,432	570.3
Scotland									
Killed	641	599	601	601	556	543	553	545	10.7
Killed or seriously injured	8,887	8,326	8,374	8,022	7,261	7,198	7,527	6,800	133.3
All Casualties	27,134	26,158	27,248	26,110	24,746	25,147	27,475	27,233	533.7
Great Britain									
Killed	5,598	5,599	5,165	5,382	5,125	5,052	5,373	5,217	9.3
Killed or seriously injured	80,130	78,658	76,145	74,134	69,418	68,543	68,531	65,658	117.6
All Casualties	321,912	324,314	317,524	321,451	311,473	322,305	341,592	341,141	611.1
Northern Ireland									
Killed	196	189	177	236	214	178	181	185	11.6
Killed or seriously injured	2,362	2,654	1,325	2,061	2,099	2,147	2,195	2,178	137.0
All Casualties	8,204	8,750	8,637	9,442	9,936	10,967	11,611	11,761	740.0
United Kingdom									
Killed	5,793	5,788	5,342	5,618	5,339	5,230	5,554	5,402	9.4
Killed or seriously injured	82,492	81,312	77,470	76,195	71,517	70,690	70,726	67,836	118.2
All Casualties	330,115	333,064	326,161	330,893	321,409	333,272	353,203	352,902	614.7

[1] In September 1984 the Metropolitan Police implemented revised standards in the assessment of serious casualties. Figures in brackets estimate casualty totals under standards prevailing since 1984. See note on page 5.

Chart 1: Casualties by region and severity: all roads: 1990

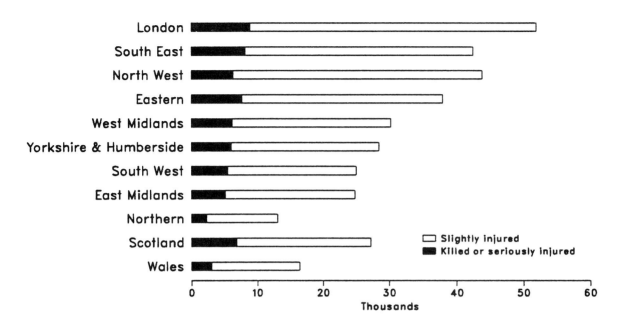

Chart 2: Casualties by built-up and non built-up roads: by region and severity: 1990

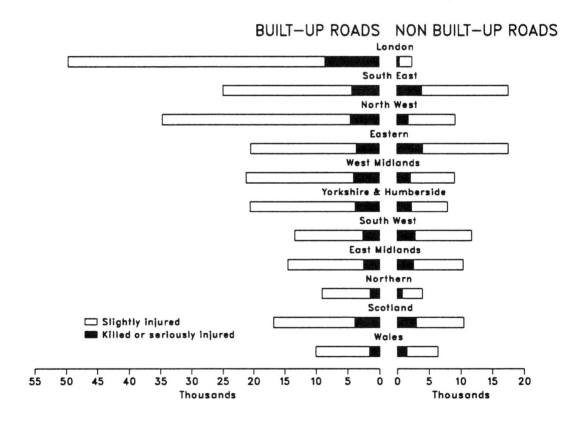

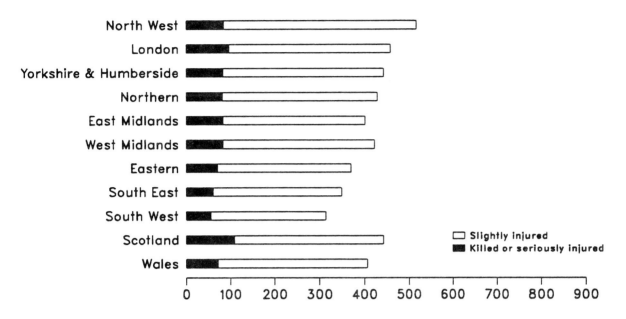

Chart 3: Child casualties per 100,000 population: by region and severity: 1990

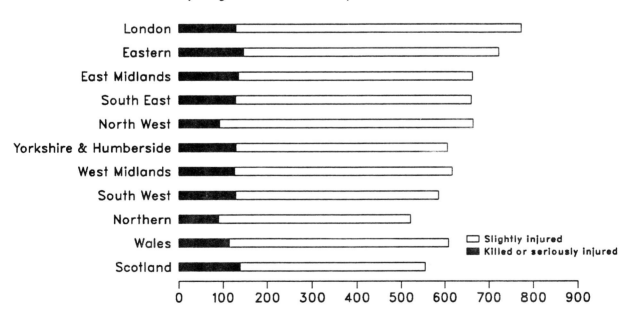

Chart 4: Adult casualties per 100,000 population: by region and severity: 1990

2 Number of casualties: by county, by type of road user: 1990

Number of casualties

	Children (0-14)	Adults (15-59)	Elderly (60+)	All[1] casualties	Pedest-rians	Pedal cyclists	Motor cyclists	Car occupants	Other road users
Avon	414	2,866	404	3,689	668	344	666	1,819	192
Bedfordshire	401	2,612	290	3,303	452	239	379	1,982	251
Berkshire	452	3,238	329	4,140	522	391	462	2,552	213
Buckinghamshire	440	3,149	274	3,935	432	267	435	2,573	228
Cambridgeshire	516	4,275	460	5,251	392	880	684	2,932	363
Cheshire	673	4,473	596	5,742	710	481	625	3,516	410
Cleveland	545	2,199	292	3,036	729	282	225	1,574	226
Cornwall	302	2,216	303	2,822	327	162	463	1,669	201
Cumbria	361	2,283	376	3,020	432	174	358	1,860	196
Derbyshire	628	4,057	437	5,330	765	324	710	3,209	322
Devon	630	4,295	650	5,575	840	348	930	3,122	335
Dorset	382	2,957	436	3,775	430	308	520	2,305	212
Durham	422	2,343	286	3,051	556	132	187	1,890	286
East Sussex	418	2,953	663	4,034	689	259	534	2,269	283
Essex	1,128	8,280	1,028	10,493	1,240	741	1,120	6,673	719
Gloucestershire	269	2,384	356	3,009	348	237	428	1,795	201
London	5,824	37,561	5,109	51,871	12,252	4,526	7,306	23,453	4,334
Greater Manchester	2,938	12,606	1,653	17,197	4,128	1,351	1,366	9,168	1,184
Hampshire	1,082	7,654	1,007	9,743	1,217	1,056	1,394	5,535	541
Hereford & Worcester	460	3,175	444	4,079	483	372	563	2,454	207
Hertfordshire	635	4,817	598	6,119	725	419	705	3,879	391
Humberside	798	3,895	794	5,487	912	839	980	2,370	386
Isle of Wight	56	424	63	543	85	48	129	255	26
Kent	943	6,353	822	8,231	1,147	566	1,342	4,720	456
Lancashire	1,292	6,020	947	8,279	1,718	630	865	4,446	620
Leicestershire	669	3,931	443	5,044	808	414	605	2,838	379
Lincolnshire	412	3,020	387	3,819	339	300	486	2,461	233
Merseyside	1,616	6,869	1,026	9,511	2,037	617	451	5,741	665
Norfolk	592	4,026	608	5,226	530	498	770	3,170	258
Northamptonshire	441	3,107	339	3,887	451	187	458	2,579	212
Northumberland	202	1,420	215	1,837	186	83	140	1,217	211
North Yorkshire	510	3,893	635	5,038	523	339	744	3,032	400
Nottinghamshire	903	4,925	944	6,772	1,148	604	886	3,501	633
Oxfordshire	323	2,828	324	3,556	337	390	526	2,054	249
Shropshire	275	2,098	287	2,660	277	181	297	1,759	146
Somerset	259	1,968	313	2,540	260	208	377	1,560	135
South Yorkshire	998	4,638	743	6,379	1,456	427	577	3,244	675
Staffordshire	909	5,832	595	7,336	944	517	736	4,655	484
Suffolk	357	2,819	405	3,581	351	352	584	2,059	235
Surrey	756	6,346	809	8,009	769	737	953	5,178	372
Tyne & Wear	938	3,546	593	5,077	1,438	345	262	2,566	466
Warwickshire	342	2,901	362	3,606	358	313	447	2,219	269
West Midlands	2,270	8,991	1,277	12,538	3,376	886	1,136	6,374	766
West Sussex	411	3,174	546	4,131	432	380	489	2,586	244
West Yorkshire	1,861	8,395	1,295	11,551	2,696	688	1,133	6,171	863
Wiltshire	343	2,905	376	3,624	369	280	462	2,239	274
England	37,396	224,717	31,139	297,476	51,284	24,122	35,895	165,223	20,952
Wales	2,228	12,422	1,777	16,432	2,721	873	1,471	10,313	1,054
Scotland	4,229	19,731	3,258	27,233	6,225	1,427	1,682	15,022	2,877
Great Britain	43,853	256,870	36,174	341,141	60,230	26,422	39,048	190,558	24,883
Northern Ireland	1,620	9,216	925	11,761	1,538	399	434	8,384	1,006
United Kingdom	45,473	266,086	37,099	352,902	61,768	26,821	39,482	198,942	25,889

[1] Includes age not reported.

20

3 Number of casualties: by county, by type of road user: 1981-1985 average

Number of casualties

	Children (0-14)	Adults (15-59)	Elderly (60+)	All[1] casualties	Pedest- rians	Pedal cyclists	Motor cyclists	Car occupants	Other road users
Avon	539	3,597	447	4,584	777	402	1,399	1,768	238
Bedfordshire	446	2,536	252	3,235	495	299	628	1,552	262
Berkshire	495	3,309	333	4,243	567	449	904	2,167	157
Buckinghamshire	408	2,769	283	3,504	409	287	700	1,940	168
Cambridgeshire	423	3,161	397	3,981	345	646	923	1,834	233
Cheshire	713	3,878	490	5,095	711	593	1,126	2,324	341
Cleveland	536	1,904	231	2,671	682	274	515	1,016	185
Cornwall	312	2,126	253	2,691	339	151	756	1,301	144
Cumbria	393	2,117	297	2,806	444	216	606	1,383	157
Derbyshire	638	3,583	439	4,933	808	405	1,207	2,098	415
Devon	679	4,424	624	5,726	845	400	1,654	2,526	302
Dorset	392	2,814	471	3,677	487	396	959	1,647	188
Durham	404	1,852	221	2,476	510	140	412	1,216	198
East Sussex	475	2,782	655	3,911	725	287	830	1,842	227
Essex	1,182	7,324	947	9,474	1,212	803	1,845	5,003	611
Gloucestershire	361	2,607	308	3,276	378	348	926	1,465	160
London	6,448	38,489	5,855	54,156	13,081	4,739	9,957	21,778	4,601
Greater Manchester	2,690	9,577	1,431	13,699	3,931	1,376	2,284	5,186	922
Hampshire	1,104	7,323	881	9,308	1,159	1,182	2,530	3,981	456
Hereford & Worcester	418	2,968	384	3,770	461	370	847	1,909	183
Hertfordshire	682	4,503	485	5,729	738	511	1,173	3,003	304
Humberside	750	3,692	491	4,934	821	727	1,377	1,620	388
Isle of Wight	91	497	74	662	107	61	206	260	28
Kent	1,097	6,923	848	8,867	1,246	744	2,291	4,139	447
Lancashire	1,268	5,287	906	7,460	1,683	666	1,458	3,188	466
Leicestershire	663	3,746	415	4,825	827	507	1,117	2,124	249
Lincolnshire	433	2,934	382	3,749	365	381	852	1,929	221
Merseyside	1,511	4,840	875	7,225	2,066	583	1,009	2,926	642
Norfolk	478	3,267	495	4,241	483	456	1,063	1,999	240
Northamptonshire	444	2,873	334	3,652	449	240	779	1,913	271
Northumberland	192	1,165	159	1,516	192	95	270	828	131
North Yorkshire	500	3,416	496	4,413	531	420	1,030	2,150	283
Nottinghamshire	888	4,462	570	5,920	1,111	609	1,362	2,381	458
Oxfordshire	332	2,734	297	3,424	362	382	798	1,663	219
Shropshire	261	1,803	211	2,275	252	185	473	1,237	129
Somerset	257	1,917	276	2,450	267	222	640	1,204	117
South Yorkshire	1,010	4,219	685	5,914	1,475	354	1,069	2,308	708
Staffordshire	914	5,096	518	6,528	983	558	1,388	3,167	432
Suffolk	415	2,826	385	3,627	397	389	961	1,696	183
Surrey	790	5,976	779	7,640	808	838	1,764	3,918	312
Tyne & Wear	946	2,988	509	4,443	1,491	334	650	1,568	400
Warwickshire	350	2,229	261	2,839	339	295	606	1,446	154
West Midlands	2,477	8,581	1,227	12,286	3,596	1,064	1,993	4,812	820
West Sussex	427	2,990	527	3,943	440	464	907	1,953	180
West Yorkshire	1,853	7,717	1,084	10,654	2,728	722	2,048	4,386	770
Wiltshire	421	3,150	377	3,948	392	358	887	2,056	256
England	38,508	208,967	28,867	280,382	52,515	25,927	59,179	123,806	18,956
Wales	2,095	10,722	1,576	14,395	2,666	857	2,566	7,211	1,094
Scotland	4,435	19,602	3,097	27,134	6,560	1,607	3,446	12,924	2,598
Great Britain	45,038	239,291	33,540	321,912	61,741	28,391	65,191	143,941	22,647
Northern Ireland[2]	1,390	6,080	731	8,204	1,648	399	765	5,398	
United Kingdom[2]	46,429	245,371	34,271	330,115	63,389	28,791	65,956	171,986	

[1] Includes age not reported.
[2] It is not possible to give separate casualty figures for car occupants and other road users for Northern Ireland for these years.

4 Total casualty rates: by county, by type of road user: 1990

Rate per 100,000 population

	Children (0-14)	Adults (15-59)	Elderly (60+)	All casualties	Pedest-rians	Pedal cyclists	Motor cyclists	Car occupants	Other road users
Avon	242	500	195	387	70	36	70	191	20
Bedfordshire	367	782	315	617	84	45	71	370	47
Berkshire	303	676	258	548	69	52	61	338	28
Buckinghamshire	338	780	254	613	67	42	68	401	36
Cambridgeshire	391	1048	369	790	59	132	103	441	55
Cheshire	366	759	320	599	74	50	65	367	43
Cleveland	479	656	282	550	132	51	41	285	41
Cornwall	363	826	261	604	70	35	99	357	43
Cumbria	415	773	342	614	88	35	73	378	40
Derbyshire	363	718	224	571	82	35	76	344	35
Devon	352	725	251	541	82	34	90	303	33
Dorset	359	802	238	573	65	47	79	350	32
Durham	380	647	226	509	93	22	31	315	48
East Sussex	365	749	326	566	97	36	75	319	40
Essex	394	901	314	684	81	48	73	435	47
Gloucestershire	277	752	304	566	65	45	81	338	38
London	457	893	389	763	180	67	108	345	64
Greater Manchester	576	804	323	664	159	52	53	354	46
Hampshire	370	810	326	630	79	68	90	358	35
Hereford & Worcester	361	772	322	603	71	55	83	363	31
Hertfordshire	338	800	301	619	73	42	71	392	40
Humberside	476	764	437	639	106	98	114	276	45
Isle of Wight	258	592	173	419	66	37	99	197	20
Kent	330	697	251	540	75	37	88	309	30
Lancashire	481	731	313	593	123	45	62	319	44
Leicestershire	379	717	257	562	90	46	67	316	42
Lincolnshire	392	849	297	646	57	51	82	416	39
Merseyside	572	802	337	659	141	43	31	398	46
Norfolk	454	924	329	696	71	66	103	422	34
Northamptonshire	380	881	304	670	78	32	79	445	37
Northumberland	359	774	328	602	61	27	46	399	69
North Yorkshire	407	880	400	694	72	47	102	417	55
Nottinghamshire	475	794	457	666	113	59	87	344	62
Oxfordshire	287	773	300	606	57	66	90	350	42
Shropshire	358	853	348	657	68	45	73	434	36
Somerset	308	725	286	546	56	45	81	336	29
South Yorkshire	416	591	274	492	112	33	45	250	52
Staffordshire	462	905	298	705	91	50	71	447	47
Suffolk	283	753	283	556	55	55	91	320	37
Surrey	418	1051	370	799	77	73	95	516	37
Tyne & Wear	444	526	245	451	128	31	23	228	41
Warwickshire	391	974	372	747	74	65	93	460	56
West Midlands	437	575	241	480	129	34	43	244	29
West Sussex	344	799	290	586	61	54	69	367	35
West Yorkshire	454	675	311	558	130	33	55	298	42
Wiltshire	317	851	335	645	66	50	82	398	49
England	415	779	313	622	107	50	75	345	44
Wales	406	731	280	570	94	30	51	358	37
Scotland	442	633	318	534	122	28	33	294	56
Great Britain	417	763	311	611	108	47	70	341	45
Northern Ireland	409	990	352	740	97	25	27	527	63
United Kingdom	416	769	312	615	108	47	69	347	45

5 Casualty indicators: by county, by type of road user: 1990

Percentage of all casualties

	Children[1] (0-14)	Adults[1] (15-59)	Elderly[1] (60+)	Pedestrians	Pedal cyclists	Motor cyclists	Car occupants	Other road users[2]
				Percentage of all casualties who are:				
Avon	11.2	77.8	11.0	18.1	9.3	18.1	49.3	5.2
Bedfordshire	12.1	79.1	8.8	13.7	7.2	11.5	60.0	7.6
Berkshire	11.2	80.6	8.2	12.6	9.4	11.2	61.6	5.1
Buckinghamshire	11.4	81.5	7.1	11.0	6.8	11.1	65.4	5.8
Cambridgeshire	9.8	81.4	8.8	7.5	16.8	13.0	55.8	6.9
Cheshire	11.7	77.9	10.4	12.4	8.4	10.9	61.2	7.1
Cleveland	18.0	72.4	9.6	24.0	9.3	7.4	51.8	7.4
Cornwall	10.7	78.6	10.7	11.6	5.7	16.4	59.1	7.1
Cumbria	12.0	75.6	12.5	14.3	5.8	11.9	61.6	6.5
Derbyshire	12.3	79.2	8.5	14.4	6.1	13.3	60.2	6.0
Devon	11.3	77.0	11.7	15.1	6.2	16.7	56.0	6.0
Dorset	10.1	78.3	11.5	11.4	8.2	13.8	61.1	5.6
Durham	13.8	76.8	9.4	18.2	4.3	6.1	61.9	9.4
East Sussex	10.4	73.2	16.4	17.1	6.4	13.2	56.2	7.0
Essex	10.8	79.3	9.9	11.8	7.1	10.7	63.6	6.9
Gloucestershire	8.9	79.2	11.8	11.6	7.9	14.2	59.7	6.7
London	12.0	77.5	10.5	23.6	8.7	14.1	45.2	8.4
Greater Manchester	17.1	73.3	9.6	24.0	7.9	7.9	53.3	6.9
Hampshire	11.1	78.6	10.3	12.5	10.8	14.3	56.8	5.6
Hereford & Worcester	11.3	77.8	10.9	11.8	9.1	13.8	60.2	5.1
Hertfordshire	10.5	79.6	9.9	11.8	6.8	11.5	63.4	6.4
Humberside	14.5	71.0	14.5	16.6	15.3	17.9	43.2	7.0
Isle of Wight	10.3	78.1	11.6	15.7	8.8	23.8	47.0	4.8
Kent	11.6	78.3	10.1	13.9	6.9	16.3	57.3	5.5
Lancashire	15.6	72.9	11.5	20.8	7.6	10.4	53.7	7.5
Leicestershire	13.3	77.9	8.8	16.0	8.2	12.0	56.3	7.5
Lincolnshire	10.8	79.1	10.1	8.9	7.9	12.7	64.4	6.1
Merseyside	17.0	72.2	10.8	21.4	6.5	4.7	60.4	7.0
Norfolk	11.3	77.0	11.6	10.1	9.5	14.7	60.7	4.9
Northamptonshire	11.3	79.9	8.7	11.6	4.8	11.8	66.3	5.5
Northumberland	11.0	77.3	11.7	10.1	4.5	7.6	66.2	11.5
North Yorkshire	10.1	77.3	12.6	10.4	6.7	14.8	60.2	7.9
Nottinghamshire	13.3	72.7	13.9	17.0	8.9	13.1	51.7	9.3
Oxfordshire	9.3	81.4	9.3	9.5	11.0	14.8	57.8	7.0
Shropshire	10.3	78.9	10.8	10.4	6.8	11.2	66.1	5.5
Somerset	10.2	77.5	12.3	10.2	8.2	14.8	61.4	5.3
South Yorkshire	15.6	72.7	11.6	22.8	6.7	9.0	50.9	10.6
Staffordshire	12.4	79.5	8.1	12.9	7.0	10.0	63.5	6.6
Suffolk	10.0	78.7	11.3	9.8	9.8	16.3	57.5	6.6
Surrey	9.6	80.2	10.2	9.6	9.2	11.9	64.7	4.6
Tyne & Wear	18.5	69.8	11.7	28.3	6.8	5.2	50.5	9.2
Warwickshire	9.5	80.5	10.0	9.9	8.7	12.4	61.5	7.5
West Midlands	18.1	71.7	10.2	26.9	7.1	9.1	50.8	6.1
West Sussex	9.9	76.8	13.2	10.5	9.2	11.8	62.6	5.9
West Yorkshire	16.1	72.7	11.2	23.3	6.0	9.8	53.4	7.5
Wiltshire	9.5	80.2	10.4	10.2	7.7	12.7	61.8	7.6
England	12.8	76.6	10.6	17.2	8.1	12.1	55.5	7.0
Wales	13.6	75.6	10.8	16.6	5.3	9.0	62.8	6.4
Scotland	15.5	72.5	12.0	22.9	5.2	6.2	55.2	10.6
Great Britain	13.0	76.2	10.7	17.7	7.7	11.4	55.9	7.3
Northern Ireland	13.8	78.4	7.9	13.1	3.4	3.7	71.3	8.6
United Kingdom	13.0	76.3	10.6	17.5	7.6	11.2	56.4	7.3

[1] Percentage of casualties of known age.
[2] Includes road user type not known.

6 Casualty changes: by county and severity: 1981-1985 to 1990

	Fatal and serious casualties			Total casualties		
	Average 1981-1985	1990	percentage change	Average 1981-1985	1990	percentage change
Avon	1,356	831	-38.7	4,584	3,689	-19.5
Bedfordshire	714	533	-25.4	3,235	3,303	2.1
Berkshire	1,095	734	-32.9	4,243	4,140	-2.4
Buckinghamshire	1,031	627	-39.2	3,504	3,935	12.3
Cambridgeshire	1,087	1,227	12.9	3,981	5,251	31.9
Cheshire	916	920	0.4	5,095	5,742	12.7
Cleveland	486	397	-18.3	2,671	3,036	13.6
Cornwall	858	611	-28.8	2,691	2,822	4.9
Cumbria	829	779	-6.0	2,806	3,020	7.6
Derbyshire	1,222	720	-41.1	4,933	5,330	8.0
Devon	1,897	1,315	-30.7	5,726	5,575	-2.6
Dorset	940	671	-28.6	3,677	3,775	2.7
Durham	703	456	-35.2	2,476	3,051	23.2
East Sussex	989	765	-22.6	3,911	4,034	3.1
Essex	2,398	1,789	-25.4	9,474	10,493	10.8
Gloucestershire	1,166	643	-44.9	3,276	3,009	-8.2
London[1]	8,230 (9,175)	8,910	8.3 -2.9	54,156	51,871	-4.2
Greater Manchester	2,362	2,075	-12.2	13,699	17,197	25.5
Hampshire	2,755	2,025	-26.5	9,308	9,743	4.7
Hereford & Worcester	1,071	827	-22.8	3,770	4,079	8.2
Hertfordshire	1,388	1,178	-15.1	5,729	6,119	6.8
Humberside	1,129	1,086	-3.8	4,934	5,487	11.2
Isle of Wight	184	133	-27.7	662	543	-18.0
Kent	2,385	1,564	-34.4	8,867	8,231	-7.2
Lancashire	1,704	1,381	-19.0	7,460	8,279	11.0
Leicestershire	1,226	791	-35.5	4,825	5,044	4.5
Lincolnshire	1,074	924	-14.0	3,749	3,819	1.9
Merseyside	1,237	1,094	-11.6	7,225	9,511	31.6
Norfolk	1,524	1,351	-11.4	4,241	5,226	23.2
Northamptonshire	1,328	1,145	-13.8	3,652	3,887	6.4
Northumberland	400	412	3.1	1,516	1,837	21.2
North Yorkshire	1,835	1,655	-9.8	4,413	5,038	14.2
Nottinghamshire	1,540	1,465	-4.9	5,920	6,772	14.4
Oxfordshire	1,067	793	-25.7	3,424	3,556	3.9
Shropshire	833	689	-17.3	2,275	2,660	16.9
Somerset	811	564	-30.4	2,450	2,540	3.7
South Yorkshire	1,320	1,002	-24.1	5,914	6,379	7.9
Staffordshire	1,442	999	-30.7	6,528	7,336	12.4
Suffolk	1,170	948	-18.9	3,627	3,581	-1.3
Surrey	1,641	1,342	-18.2	7,640	8,009	4.8
Tyne & Wear	1,048	1,006	-4.0	4,443	5,077	14.3
Warwickshire	1,059	919	-13.2	2,839	3,606	27.0
West Midlands	3,452	2,702	-21.7	12,286	12,538	2.1
West Sussex	922	799	-13.3	3,943	4,131	4.8
West Yorkshire	2,547	2,235	-12.2	10,654	11,551	8.4
Wiltshire	1,019	789	-22.6	3,948	3,624	-8.2
England	67,388	55,821	-17.2	280,382	297,476	6.1
Wales	3,855	3,037	-21.2	14,395	16,432	14.2
Scotland	8,887	6,800	-23.5	27,134	27,233	0.4
Great Britain	80,130	65,658	-18.1	321,912	341,141	6.0
Northern Ireland	2,362	2,178	-7.8	8,204	11,761	43.4
United Kingdom	82,492	67,836	-17.8	330,115	352,902	6.9

[1] In September 1984 the Metropolitan Police implemented revised standards in the assessment of serious casualties. Figures in brackets estimate casualty totals under standards prevailing since 1984. See note on page 5.

7 Number of Casualties: by road class, region[1] and severity: 1990

Number of casualties

	Motorways	Built up				Non built up				All roads[2]
		Trunk	Principal	Other	Total	Trunk	Principal	Other	Total	
Northern										
Killed	4	2	53	76	131	34	48	29	111	246
Killed or Seriously Injured	18	9	513	955	1,477	187	328	261	776	2,271
All Casualties	167	98	3,236	5,704	9,038	903	1,646	1,244	3,793	13,001
Yorkshire and Humberside										
Killed	15	19	87	124	230	49	91	43	183	428
Killed or Seriously Injured	144	147	1,305	2,295	3,747	557	809	718	2,084	5,978
All Casualties	687	760	7,249	12,470	20,479	1,879	2,781	2,601	7,261	28,455
East Midlands										
Killed	12	19	63	94	176	111	127	85	323	513
Killed or Seriously Injured	135	213	778	1,511	2,502	676	945	781	2,402	5,045
All Casualties	758	1,097	4,914	8,459	14,470	2,770	3,602	3,241	9,613	24,852
Eastern										
Killed	37	16	66	102	184	112	141	134	387	608
Killed or Seriously Injured	279	154	1,051	2,389	3,594	896	1,223	1,660	3,779	7,653
All Casualties	1,840	835	6,430	13,113	20,378	3,602	5,278	6,804	15,684	37,908
South East										
Killed	47	11	97	122	230	105	180	137	422	699
Killed or Seriously Injured	400	131	1,607	2,496	4,234	696	1,430	1,393	3,519	8,155
All Casualties	2,023	759	9,768	14,359	24,886	2,933	6,343	6,188	15,464	42,387
London										
Killed	5	74	197	104	375	21	-	7	28	408
Killed or Seriously Injured	61	869	4,264	3,354	8,487	258	24	80	362	8,910
All Casualties	496	5,153	24,224	20,167	49,544	1,287	129	415	1,831	51,871
South West										
Killed	14	6	75	84	165	63	134	92	289	468
Killed or Seriously Injured	150	78	883	1,625	2,586	480	1,199	1,009	2,688	5,424
All Casualties	719	415	4,688	8,199	13,302	1,879	4,872	4,259	11,010	25,034
West Midlands										
Killed	31	13	106	124	243	51	82	71	204	478
Killed or Seriously Injured	218	162	1,458	2,409	4,029	504	630	755	1,889	6,136
All Casualties	1,236	846	7,854	12,450	21,150	2,125	2,694	3,014	7,833	30,219
North West										
Killed	46	18	165	156	339	80	69	41	190	575
Killed or Seriously Injured	306	157	1,857	2,476	4,490	411	555	487	1,453	6,249
All Casualties	2,040	1,073	14,726	18,818	34,617	1,989	2,750	2,348	7,087	43,749
England										
Killed	211	178	909	986	2,073	626	872	639	2,137	4,423
Killed or Seriously Injured	1,711	1,920	13,716	19,510	35,146	4,665	7,143	7,144	18,952	55,821
All Casualties	9,966	11,036	83,089	113,739	207,864	19,367	30,095	30,114	79,576	297,476
Wales										
Killed	7	9	43	56	108	53	63	18	134	249
Killed or Seriously Injured	60	110	517	927	1,554	501	505	417	1,423	3,037
All Casualties	349	627	3,429	5,979	10,035	2,063	2,117	1,868	6,048	16,432
Scotland[3]										
Killed	11	11	92	116	219	146	109	60	315	545
Killed or Seriously Injured	101	177	1,315	2,354	3,846	1,073	971	809	2,853	6,800
All Casualties	526	780	5,842	10,177	16,799	3,373	3,545	2,990	9,908	27,233
Great Britain[3]										
Killed	229	198	1,044	1,158	2,400	825	1,044	717	2,586	5,217
Killed or Seriously Injured	1,872	2,207	15,548	22,791	40,546	6,239	8,619	8,370	23,228	65,658
All Casualties	10,841	12,443	92,360	129,895	234,698	24,803	35,757	34,972	95,532	341,141

1 Casualty data by road class are not available for Northern Ireland.
2 Includes speed limit not reported.
3 19 accidents in Scotland, originally recorded as motorway accidents, have been re-allocated as A road accidents. There were 28 casualties in these accidents.

8 Casualty rates per 100 million vehicle kilometres: by road class, region[1] and severity: 1988-1990 average

Rate per 100 million vehicle kilometres

| | | A roads | | | | All A roads | All main roads |
| | Motorways | Built up | | Non built up | | | |
		Trunk	Principal	Trunk	Principal		
Northern							
Fatal	0.5	2.0	2.1	1.3	1.6	1.6	1.5
Fatal or serious	2.8	17.2	21.1	7.1	11.9	13.2	12.4
All severities	23.2	112.6	125.9	32.4	56.4	70.5	66.6
Yorkshire and Humberside							
Fatal	0.3	2.5	1.7	1.4	2.2	1.8	1.4
Fatal or serious	2.6	24.3	23.1	13.9	20.3	19.8	15.6
All severities	13.3	116.9	121.5	44.5	71.9	86.8	68.6
East Midlands							
Fatal	0.5	1.9	1.6	2.0	2.4	2.0	1.8
Fatal or serious	4.3	24.6	22.8	13.1	19.7	18.3	15.7
All severities	20.9	127.7	130.8	50.7	74.7	83.3	71.5
Eastern							
Fatal	0.4	1.9	1.3	1.2	1.9	1.4	1.1
Fatal or serious	3.0	24.0	20.3	9.8	17.0	15.1	11.7
All severities	19.3	121.3	117.4	38.4	69.2	70.1	55.8
South East							
Fatal	0.5	1.7	1.1	1.3	1.7	1.4	1.1
Fatal or serious	3.5	20.2	19.1	8.6	15.1	14.6	11.5
All severities	16.7	99.0	104.7	34.6	61.8	68.7	54.1
London							
Fatal	0.4	2.3	2.0	1.1	2.3	1.9	1.8
Fatal or serious	4.8	28.4	42.7	10.9	14.2	34.9	33.0
All severities	39.3	162.5	234.7	53.2	70.8	192.1	182.2
South West							
Fatal	0.4	1.0	1.1	1.2	1.7	1.4	1.2
Fatal or serious	3.2	13.5	16.7	8.5	15.9	13.9	11.7
All severities	13.6	72.8	84.3	31.7	61.2	59.9	50.4
West Midlands							
Fatal	0.3	2.2	1.7	1.5	1.7	1.7	1.2
Fatal or serious	2.3	22.0	22.1	13.0	14.9	17.9	12.6
All severities	12.9	110.7	112.8	50.5	61.8	83.4	59.7
North West							
Fatal	0.5	2.1	1.8	1.7	1.6	1.8	1.3
Fatal or serious	2.5	22.0	18.6	11.2	12.3	15.8	11.1
All severities	17.8	144.3	143.2	54.1	59.9	106.3	74.9
England							
Fatal	0.4	2.0	1.6	1.4	1.8	1.6	1.3
Fatal or serious	3.0	24.0	24.1	10.5	16.0	17.9	14.1
All severities	17.0	131.1	137.9	41.6	64.6	89.1	71.0
Wales							
Fatal	0.3	1.1	1.6	1.4	1.7	1.5	1.4
Fatal or serious	3.3	19.2	20.2	13.7	17.3	16.9	15.0
All severities	17.0	98.1	126.4	55.4	68.0	81.9	72.7
Scotland[2]							
Fatal	0.5	1.7	1.8	2.3	2.1	2.1	1.8
Fatal or serious	4.0	23.5	30.0	16.5	20.3	21.6	19.0
All severities	16.1	96.2	124.6	48.7	63.1	75.6	66.6
Great Britain[2]							
Fatal	0.4	1.9	1.6	1.5	1.9	1.7	1.4
Fatal or serious	3.1	23.7	24.3	11.4	16.5	18.2	14.6
All severities	17.0	126.2	136.5	43.3	64.7	87.5	70.7

[1] Traffic data and casualty data in this breakdown are not available for Northern Ireland.
[2] 19 accidents in Scotland, originally recorded as motorway accidents, have been re-allocated as A road accidents. There were 28 casualties in these accidents.

9 Accident rates per 100 million vehicle kilometres: by road class, region[1] and severity: 1988-1990 average

Rate per 100 million vehicle kilometres

| | Motorways | A roads | | | | All A roads | All main roads |
| | | Built up | | Non built up | | | |
		Trunk	Principal	Trunk	Principal		
Northern							
Fatal	0.4	2.0	2.0	1.1	1.4	1.5	1.4
Fatal or serious	2.4	14.1	19.4	5.1	9.1	11.0	10.3
All severities	14.4	77.0	98.4	19.6	35.0	49.9	47.0
Yorkshire and Humberside							
Fatal	0.2	2.4	1.7	1.2	2.0	1.7	1.3
Fatal or serious	1.9	20.4	20.6	9.6	14.4	15.9	12.4
All severities	8.5	89.7	88.8	26.2	44.4	62.7	49.3
East Midlands							
Fatal	0.5	1.7	1.5	1.6	2.1	1.8	1.5
Fatal or serious	3.0	21.1	20.4	8.9	14.0	14.2	12.1
All severities	12.9	98.4	103.3	30.6	46.4	58.1	49.6
Eastern							
Fatal	0.3	1.8	1.2	1.0	1.6	1.3	1.0
Fatal or serious	2.3	20.7	18.5	7.1	12.6	12.0	9.3
All severities	12.2	95.1	93.8	23.6	43.6	49.3	38.9
South East							
Fatal	0.4	1.5	1.1	1.1	1.5	1.2	1.0
Fatal or serious	2.6	16.9	17.6	6.2	11.3	12.0	9.4
All severities	10.7	75.7	85.4	21.6	40.5	50.4	39.3
London							
Fatal	0.4	2.2	2.0	1.1	1.8	1.9	1.8
Fatal or serious	4.1	25.3	39.5	9.2	11.0	32.0	30.2
All severities	27.3	133.1	201.5	38.0	56.5	162.5	153.7
South West							
Fatal	0.3	0.9	1.1	1.0	1.5	1.2	1.0
Fatal or serious	2.2	12.4	15.2	6.1	11.7	11.1	9.3
All severities	7.9	57.3	68.7	19.5	38.5	42.5	35.4
West Midlands							
Fatal	0.2	2.1	1.6	1.3	1.6	1.6	1.1
Fatal or serious	1.7	18.8	19.4	9.5	11.0	14.7	10.3
All severities	8.1	82.1	88.1	31.9	40.0	60.8	43.1
North West							
Fatal	0.4	1.9	1.8	1.3	1.4	1.6	1.2
Fatal or serious	1.8	18.9	17.0	8.1	9.2	13.5	9.4
All severities	11.1	103.2	109.9	33.1	38.3	77.8	54.1
England							
Fatal	0.3	1.9	1.6	1.2	1.6	1.5	1.2
Fatal or serious	2.2	20.9	21.9	7.5	11.8	14.9	11.7
All severities	10.7	102.9	111.8	25.7	41.1	66.6	52.5
Wales							
Fatal	0.3	1.0	1.5	1.2	1.6	1.4	1.2
Fatal or serious	2.4	15.7	17.3	9.2	12.3	12.8	11.4
All severities	11.0	73.0	96.3	32.2	42.2	55.8	49.5
Scotland[2]							
Fatal	0.5	1.6	1.7	1.9	1.9	1.8	1.6
Fatal or serious	3.1	21.3	27.3	11.0	14.9	17.1	15.0
All severities	10.1	74.7	100.2	28.2	39.1	52.9	46.4
Great Britain[2]							
Fatal	0.3	1.8	1.6	1.3	1.6	1.5	1.2
Fatal or serious	2.3	20.6	22.1	8.0	12.1	15.0	11.9
All severities	10.7	98.8	110.3	26.4	40.9	64.7	51.9

[1] Traffic data and accident data in this breakdown are not available for Northern Ireland.
[2] 19 accidents in Scotland, originally recorded as motorway accidents, have been re-allocated as A road accidents. There were 28 casualties in these accidents.

10 Accident indices[1] : by month, severity and region: accidents by severity and region: 1990

Index/number

	Jan	Feb	Mar	Apr	May	Jun	Jul	Aug	Sep	Oct	Nov	Dec	All accidents
Northern													
Fatal & serious	110	93	97	83	98	92	107	100	113	111	109	88	1,950
All	104	92	94	91	95	102	99	98	99	107	112	107	9,564
Yorkshire and Humberside													
Fatal & serious	105	96	96	97	101	90	103	97	104	102	109	100	5,004
All	102	92	94	92	102	95	103	101	99	108	110	102	21,542
East Midlands													
Fatal & serious	112	84	92	91	106	95	110	97	109	104	107	92	4,075
All	105	93	94	91	104	98	104	94	104	106	109	97	18,101
Eastern													
Fatal & serious	113	91	91	96	89	101	101	104	102	110	114	89	6,416
All	109	91	96	93	97	99	99	97	104	102	116	96	27,827
South East													
Fatal & serious	106	99	94	103	100	97	96	99	102	104	109	90	6,887
All	102	94	95	97	101	101	101	96	101	105	110	97	31,975
London													
Fatal & serious	100	102	111	111	100	96	102	88	96	106	99	89	8,140
All	99	97	104	101	101	98	103	96	99	107	105	90	43,835
South West													
Fatal & serious	104	96	106	88	108	92	103	105	101	102	108	89	4,496
All	100	91	92	96	105	107	109	100	101	104	104	90	18,538
West Midlands													
Fatal & serious	107	101	96	91	102	96	100	98	97	115	111	87	5,141
All	107	96	93	96	101	100	98	94	105	111	106	93	22,565
North West													
Fatal & serious	99	94	87	97	102	96	95	106	107	97	111	110	5,418
All	99	94	93	97	98	101	99	102	100	110	107	98	32,494
England													
Fatal & serious	105	96	97	97	100	95	101	99	102	105	108	93	47,527
All	102	94	96	96	101	100	102	97	101	107	108	96	226,441
Wales													
Fatal & serious	96	95	106	96	105	101	103	113	102	86	109	87	2,435
All	89	90	99	96	99	101	107	110	107	100	104	98	11,826
Scotland													
Fatal & serious	97	94	94	91	95	94	106	107	106	103	111	101	5,730
All	94	92	96	89	102	100	96	109	104	104	109	103	20,174
Great Britain													
Fatal & serious	104	96	97	97	100	96	102	100	102	104	108	93	55,692
All	101	94	96	95	101	100	101	99	102	106	108	96	258,441
Northern Ireland													
Fatal & serious	120	97	93	96	88	95	87	86	95	128	113	102	1,502
All	109	106	98	99	96	103	92	107	97	112	93	88	7,159
United Kingdom													
Fatal & serious	105	96	97	97	100	96	101	100	102	105	109	93	57,194
All	101	94	96	96	101	100	101	99	102	106	108	96	265,600

[1] The base(=100) is the average number of accidents per month for the region.

11 Accidents on motorways: by carriageway type, junction, number of lanes, region[1] and severity: 1990

Number of accidents

| | Junction | | | Non-junction | | |
| | Number of lanes | | Circular section of roundabouts | Number of lanes | | Total[2] |
	2	3+		2	3+	
Northern						
Fatal or serious	2	2	1	11	-	16
All severities	14	7	9	65	6	106
Yorkshire and Humberside						
Fatal or serious	9	10	1	13	63	104
All severities	41	34	38	67	233	443
East Midlands						
Fatal or serious	-	8	5	1	81	98
All severities	5	27	26	10	383	470
Eastern						
Fatal or serious	3	6	2	20	153	199
All severities	26	66	20	132	836	1,142
South East						
Fatal or serious	3	14	10	36	206	302
All severities	43	46	52	185	790	1,262
London						
Fatal or serious	4	4	1	11	28	48
All severities	21	39	39	62	174	338
of which:						
Inner London						
Fatal or serious	-	-	1	-	1	2
All severities	2	3	12	3	5	25
Outer London						
Fatal or serious	4	4	-	11	27	46
All severities	19	36	27	59	169	313
South West						
Fatal or serious	4	7	1	2	81	102
All severities	14	16	10	29	319	425
West Midlands						
Fatal or serious	4	10	-	20	100	141
All severities	22	41	4	129	497	726
North West						
Fatal or serious	5	13	2	14	160	211
All severities	53	95	67	107	820	1,241
England						
Fatal or serious	34	74	23	128	872	1,221
All severities	239	371	265	786	4,058	6,153
Wales						
Fatal or serious	2	3	1	20	15	42
All severities	15	9	5	92	92	215
Scotland[3]						
Fatal or serious	12	10	1	38	23	84
All severities	42	25	2	131	119	319
Great Britain[3]						
Fatal or serious	48	87	25	186	910	1,347
All severities	296	405	272	1,009	4,269	6,687

[1] Accident data are not available in this breakdown for Northern Ireland.
[2] Includes unknown carriageway type and slip roads.
[3] 19 accidents in Scotland, originally recorded as motorway accidents, have been re-allocated as A road accidents.

12 Accidents on trunk 'A' roads: by carriageway type, junction, number of lanes, region[1] and severity: 1990

Number of accidents

	Dual carriageway					Single carriageway							Circular section of round-abouts[5]	All trunk A roads[6]
	Junction Number of lanes[2]		Non-junction Number of lanes[2]			Junction Number of lanes[3]			Non-junction Number of lanes[3]					
	2	3+	2	3+	All	2[4]	3	4+	2[4]	3	4+	All		
Northern														
Fatal or serious	23	3	34	1	61	16	4	-	47	1	-	68	7	136
All severities	98	6	173	22	299	79	9	5	149	6	-	248	70	619
Yorkshire and Humberside														
Fatal or serious	76	2	110	4	192	132	6	7	143	7	2	297	22	513
All severities	240	12	353	12	617	433	24	36	419	22	9	943	143	1,713
East Midlands														
Fatal or serious	74	3	89	2	168	181	7	2	254	10	4	458	29	657
All severities	266	25	333	7	631	755	47	22	821	27	9	1,681	213	2,531
Eastern														
Fatal or serious	105	8	192	20	325	164	12	5	247	7	1	436	39	801
All severities	333	25	703	66	1,127	676	42	22	730	19	5	1,494	292	2,920
South East														
Fatal or serious	77	10	132	26	245	124	11	1	168	2	2	308	40	595
All severities	316	83	490	138	1,027	470	25	9	513	13	12	1,042	315	2,381
London														
Fatal or serious	132	224	106	145	607	181	13	69	57	5	19	344	39	991
All severities	794	907	489	631	2,821	1,050	78	398	341	27	105	1,999	325	5,149
of which:														
Inner London														
Fatal or serious	46	84	25	46	201	90	4	45	26	2	12	179	4	384
All severities	253	304	109	169	835	580	31	287	173	10	66	1,147	42	2,024
Outer London														
Fatal or serious	86	140	81	99	406	91	9	24	31	3	7	165	35	607
All severities	541	603	380	462	1,986	470	47	111	168	17	39	852	283	3,125
South West														
Fatal or serious	32	1	56	6	95	103	11	-	148	22	1	285	31	411
All severities	128	14	215	16	373	393	29	5	455	56	1	939	166	1,479
West Midlands														
Fatal or serious	59	5	81	9	154	133	12	1	178	2	-	326	40	521
All severities	240	24	272	27	563	563	67	10	548	11	2	1,201	241	2,014
North West														
Fatal or serious	47	20	44	9	120	95	4	14	167	1	11	292	19	432
All severities	234	117	182	39	572	477	33	89	521	5	39	1,164	186	1,937
England														
Fatal or serious	625	276	844	222	1,967	1,129	80	99	1,409	57	40	2,814	266	5,057
All severities	2,649	1,213	3,210	958	8,030	4,896	354	596	4,497	186	182	10,711	1,951	20,743
Wales														
Fatal or serious	18	4	44	1	67	123	6	-	224	17	-	370	7	445
All severities	106	7	203	6	322	471	37	-	735	52	-	1,295	52	1,675
Scotland[7]														
Fatal or serious	73	7	139	7	226	178	9	4	414	8	17	630	11	867
All severities	218	25	406	22	671	596	16	21	1,090	16	41	1,780	70	2,527
Great Britain[7]														
Fatal or serious	716	287	1,027	230	2,260	1,430	95	103	2,047	82	57	3,814	284	6,369
All severities	2,973	1,245	3,819	986	9,023	5,963	407	617	6,322	254	223	13,786	2,073	24,945

[1] Accident data in this breakdown are not available for Northern Ireland.
[2] Number of lanes in each direction.
[3] Number of lanes in both directions.
[4] Includes one way streets
[5] These are classified as junction accidents.
[6] Includes unknown carriageway type and single track roads.
[7] 19 accidents in Scotland, originally recorded as motorway accidents, have been re-allocated as A road accidents.

30

13 Accidents on principal 'A' roads: by carriageway type, junction, number of lanes, region[1] and severity: 1990

Number of accidents

	Dual carriageway					Single carriageway							Circular section of round-abouts[5]	All principal A roads[6]
	Junction Number of lanes[2]		Non-junction Number of lanes[2]			Junction Number of lanes[3]			Non-junction Number of lanes[3]					
	2	3+	2	3+	All	2[4]	3	4+	2[4]	3	4+	All		
Northern														
Fatal or serious	65	5	78	9	157	243	12	27	215	8	14	519	37	713
All severities	342	25	263	27	657	1,305	68	151	862	24	66	2,476	370	3,518
Yorkshire and Humberside														
Fatal or serious	146	39	97	23	305	685	5	33	536	25	8	1,292	76	1,727
All severities	695	182	400	71	1,348	3,065	242	216	1,847	77	49	5,496	515	7,400
East Midlands														
Fatal or serious	82	13	76	3	174	516	21	36	535	10	13	1,131	39	1,347
All severities	438	90	244	14	786	2,674	114	198	1,925	24	47	4,982	273	6,055
Eastern														
Fatal or serious	99	6	104	9	218	756	40	15	717	14	5	1,547	129	1,901
All severities	488	55	433	41	1,017	3,583	165	92	2,498	69	21	6,428	980	8,477
South East														
Fatal or serious	190	30	170	18	408	951	59	39	921	25	20	2,015	116	2,554
All severities	864	154	672	66	1,756	5,036	242	227	3,466	100	73	9,144	1,018	12,066
London														
Fatal or serious	350	64	123	28	565	1,981	82	362	764	11	121	3,321	73	3,959
All severities	1,902	375	584	126	2,987	11,024	370	1,815	3,460	85	561	17,315	575	20,891
of which: Inner London														
Fatal or serious	211	50	53	18	332	932	53	245	316	8	80	1,634	28	1,994
All severities	1,224	291	326	89	1,930	5,493	242	1,249	1,449	52	396	8,881	235	11,055
Outer London														
Fatal or serious	139	14	70	10	233	1,049	29	117	448	3	41	1,687	45	1,965
All severities	678	84	258	37	1,057	5,531	128	566	2,011	33	165	8,434	340	9,836
South West														
Fatal or serious	81	20	74	9	184	623	32	12	716	17	4	1,404	77	1,667
All severities	346	91	255	40	732	2,839	123	58	2,430	72	18	5,540	545	6,852
West Midlands														
Fatal or serious	167	53	150	26	396	646	38	66	479	11	31	1,271	74	1,755
All severities	806	261	482	79	1,628	3056	177	344	1,831	49	127	5,584	565	7,829
North West														
Fatal or serious	166	102	87	45	400	857	52	137	543	10	46	1,645	39	2,100
All severities	1,245	637	469	212	2,563	5,607	313	902	2,433	50	232	9,537	532	12,829
England														
Fatal or serious	1,346	332	959	170	2,807	7,258	341	727	5,426	131	262	14,145	660	17,723
All severities	7,126	1,870	3,802	676	13,474	38,189	1,814	4,003	20,752	550	1,194	66,502	5,373	85,917
Wales														
Fatal or serious	32	9	25	5	71	282	30	17	352	11	7	699	19	795
All severities	235	72	144	18	469	1,430	118	92	1,435	45	41	3,161	198	3,889
Scotland[7]														
Fatal or serious	107	29	143	21	300	557	19	100	815	6	57	1,554	53	1,937
All severities	496	119	437	64	1,116	2,249	93	386	2,509	21	199	5,457	262	6,901
Great Britain[7]														
Fatal or serious	1,485	370	1,127	196	3,178	8,097	390	844	6,593	148	326	16,398	732	20,455
All severities	7,857	2,061	4,383	758	15,059	41,868	2,025	4,481	24,696	616	1,434	75,120	5,833	96,707

[1] Accident data in this breakdown are not available for Northern Ireland.
[2] Number of lanes in each direction.
[3] Number of lanes in both directions.
[4] Includes one way streets
[5] These are classified as junction accidents.
[6] Includes unknown carriageway type and single track roads.
[7] 19 accidents in Scotland, originally recorded as motorway accidents, have been re-allocated as A road accidents.

14 Accidents: by road class, severity, region and county: 1981–85 average, 1989, 1990

Number

	Motorways			Trunk A roads			Principal A roads			All roads		
	Fatal	Fatal or serious	All severities	Fatal	Fatal or serious	All severities	Fatal	Fatal or serious	All severities	Fatal	Fatal or serious	All severities
Northern Region												
1981-85	2	15	56	21	133	478	88	813	2,997	205	2,255	8,570
1989	1	18	120	32	162	634	72	725	3,428	195	1,988	9,414
1990	4	16	106	30	136	619	97	713	3,518	232	1,950	9,564
Cleveland[1]												
1981-85	-	-	-	4	19	97	18	174	770	42	423	2,137
1989	-	-	-	7	19	120	18	140	920	38	321	2,373
1990	-	-	-	4	17	122	24	160	979	42	343	2,405
Durham												
1981-85	2	10	35	7	40	110	24	195	585	55	577	1,801
1989	1	14	81	7	40	161	15	135	624	53	453	2,027
1990	4	7	59	13	37	171	22	130	642	66	380	2,067
Northumberland[1]												
1981-85	-	-	-	7	45	163	11	87	280	35	313	1,043
1989	-	-	-	16	74	220	12	109	399	38	323	1,176
1990	-	-	-	12	69	219	16	88	393	45	308	1,193
Tyne and Wear												
1981-85	-	5	21	2	29	107	36	357	1,361	73	942	3,588
1989	-	4	39	2	29	133	27	341	1,485	66	891	3,838
1990	-	9	47	1	13	107	35	335	1,504	79	919	3,899
Yorkshire and Humberside Region												
1981-85	14	78	306	65	541	1,498	196	2,053	6,932	463	5,714	20,018
1989	8	80	391	78	538	1,691	178	1,789	7,679	440	5,090	21,694
1990	11	104	443	63	513	1,713	170	1,727	7,400	405	5,004	21,542
Humberside												
1981-85	2	10	33	8	72	243	28	308	1,201	73	996	3,894
1989	2	16	56	6	58	250	27	331	1,446	76	1,016	4,398
1990	1	19	43	3	46	223	24	287	1,367	63	983	4,356
North Yorkshire												
1981-85	-	3	8	24	239	467	29	474	1,048	82	1,423	3,128
1989	-	2	9	40	273	634	31	427	1,147	114	1,402	3,621
1990	-	2	8	30	284	672	38	380	1,041	92	1,244	3,405
South Yorkshire												
1981-85	4	26	110	10	75	250	42	420	1,654	103	1,123	4,631
1989	3	31	136	7	61	270	34	335	1,828	76	890	4,924
1990	5	27	157	11	58	256	34	304	1,721	87	846	4,882
West Yorkshire												
1981-85	7	39	155	23	155	538	96	851	3,030	205	2,172	8,365
1989	3	31	190	25	146	537	86	696	3,258	174	1,782	8,751
1990	5	56	235	19	125	562	74	756	3,271	163	1,931	8,899
East Midlands Region												
1981-85	15	129	390	97	792	2,350	158	1,770	5,721	443	5,334	17,379
1989	13	115	443	134	708	2,643	153	1,440	6,175	464	4,316	18,351
1990	11	98	470	106	657	2,531	170	1,347	6,055	444	4,075	18,101
Derbyshire												
1981-85	2	18	69	20	159	545	34	339	1,130	97	1,057	3,743
1989	3	14	78	33	130	590	35	216	1,160	106	682	3,733
1990	2	11	103	14	117	573	28	192	1,151	76	621	3,815
Leicestershire												
1981-85	6	24	93	16	115	360	32	330	1,198	93	1,042	3,702
1989	4	32	125	21	93	367	33	230	1,231	90	728	3,690
1990	4	26	132	16	67	390	26	208	1,229	93	673	3,782
Lincolnshire[1]												
1981-85	-	-	-	20	160	454	29	294	932	76	852	2,683
1989	-	-	-	28	148	531	29	257	963	79	708	2,820
1990	-	-	-	30	133	491	41	260	948	94	698	2,635

[1] This county contains no motorways.

14 Accidents: by road class, severity, region and county: 1981-85 average, 1989, 1990 (cont.)

Number

	Motorways			Trunk A roads			Principal A roads			All roads		
	Fatal	Fatal or serious	All severities	Fatal	Fatal or serious	All severities	Fatal	Fatal or serious	All severities	Fatal	Fatal or serious	All severities
Northamptonshire												
1981-85	6	75	190	18	182	434	22	381	1,011	69	1,025	2,673
1989	4	56	188	30	160	438	37	348	1,135	94	959	2,960
1990	5	55	183	17	158	407	38	304	1,122	77	823	2,766
Nottinghamshire												
1981-85	1	11	38	22	175	557	41	426	1,450	108	1,359	4,577
1989	2	13	52	22	177	717	19	389	1,686	95	1,239	5,148
1990	-	6	52	29	182	670	37	383	1,605	104	1,260	5,103
Eastern Region												
1981-85	20	153	560	104	876	2,591	199	2,488	8,215	543	7,727	25,186
1989	27	218	1,163	112	840	3,107	207	1,984	8,813	566	6,648	28,883
1990	28	199	1,142	118	801	2,920	180	1,901	8,477	547	6,416	27,827
Bedfordshire												
1981-85	4	29	109	10	94	345	17	160	622	50	600	2,444
1989	6	27	151	13	92	453	18	122	644	53	481	2,571
1990	-	14	124	12	85	394	14	126	645	47	462	2,398
Buckinghamshire												
1981-85	5	38	120	3	36	110	27	318	1,001	63	843	2,617
1989	5	42	223	1	30	134	25	198	1,020	55	568	2,881
1990	6	30	212	2	33	124	28	198	1,021	55	546	2,875
Cambridgeshire												
1981-85	1	5	19	23	158	462	25	303	1,009	75	908	2,979
1989	-	6	36	21	185	635	34	326	1,236	81	1,009	3,791
1990	-	4	22	32	189	652	28	314	1,220	85	1,026	3,895
Essex												
1981-85	3	29	109	11	97	321	53	675	2,398	125	2,032	6,976
1989	4	47	302	18	87	440	48	535	2,605	140	1,714	8,313
1990	6	52	291	19	89	440	46	446	2,302	131	1,527	7,703
Hertfordshire												
1981-85	7	53	203	16	121	404	30	393	1,469	84	1,177	4,316
1989	12	96	451	10	86	378	28	251	1,295	82	977	4,673
1990	16	99	493	9	87	375	25	274	1,328	86	1,003	4,550
Norfolk[1]												
1981-85	-	-	-	21	190	461	27	360	910	82	1,207	3,110
1989	-	-	-	27	212	621	34	329	1,131	94	1,168	3,881
1990	-	-	-	27	197	561	25	301	1,086	85	1,091	3,744
Suffolk[1]												
1981-85	-	-	-	20	179	488	19	280	805	64	960	2,744
1989	-	-	-	22	148	446	20	223	882	61	731	2,773
1990	-	-	-	17	121	374	14	242	875	58	761	2,662
South East Region												
1981-85	29	205	652	109	800	2,453	282	3,500	12,091	677	9,327	32,192
1989	49	286	1,248	103	682	2,701	258	2,726	11,924	643	7,448	32,710
1990	38	302	1,262	89	595	2,381	247	2,554	12,066	616	6,887	31,975
Berkshire												
1981-85	10	69	215	7	61	195	24	321	1,167	71	942	3,263
1989	9	58	280	6	33	148	21	290	1,169	61	780	3,226
1990	10	79	288	7	30	164	17	213	1,109	53	635	3,108
East Sussex[1]												
1981-85	-	-	-	10	78	232	31	347	1,163	66	838	2,997
1989	-	-	-	4	65	219	35	300	1,318	57	688	3,124
1990	-	-	-	12	53	183	37	292	1,249	73	660	3,087
Hampshire												
1981-85	4	36	109	21	160	437	50	792	2,416	140	2,320	7,227
1989	11	65	237	17	116	458	49	618	2,554	138	1,843	7,672
1990	7	67	252	17	108	409	52	557	2,434	151	1,692	7,481

[1] This county contains no motorways.

33

Number

	Motorways			Trunk A roads			Principal A roads			All roads		
	Fatal	Fatal or serious	All severities	Fatal	Fatal or serious	All severities	Fatal	Fatal or serious	All severities	Fatal	Fatal or serious	All severities
Isle of Wight[1]												
1981-85	-	-	-	-	-	-	4	70	214	8	155	495
1989	-	-	-	-	-	-	3	57	203	7	136	489
1990	-	-	-	-	-	-	3	46	194	6	113	409
Kent												
1981-85	7	49	162	21	175	539	63	779	2,543	142	2,053	6,819
1989	8	47	224	24	170	635	61	596	2,404	137	1,518	6,331
1990	7	44	210	19	162	649	50	504	2,336	122	1,378	6,233
Oxfordshire												
1981-85	1	6	12	24	164	521	26	279	801	71	871	2,531
1989	2	3	18	30	141	597	17	173	779	68	601	2,618
1990	-	4	18	20	110	386	23	235	1,013	59	639	2,561
Surrey												
1981-85	7	43	144	10	62	224	52	613	2,618	109	1,391	5,870
1989	18	109	465	4	51	266	39	459	2,370	98	1,228	6,229
1990	13	105	476	6	45	246	29	466	2,552	83	1,131	6,075
West Sussex												
1981-85	-	2	9	16	102	306	31	299	1,170	70	757	2,990
1989	1	4	24	18	106	378	33	233	1,127	77	654	3,021
1990	1	3	18	8	87	344	36	241	1,179	69	639	3,021
London[2]												
1981-85	6	35	266	56	413	2,489	301	4,269	25,584	521	7,588	45,274
1989	4	54	310	102	1,085	5,214	213	4,098	21,677	440	8,559	44,754
1990	5	48	338	90	991	5,149	191	3,959	20,891	393	8,140	43,835
Inner London												
1981-85[3]	N/A	N/A	N/A	N/A	N/A	N/A	N/A	N/A	N/A	212	3,383	20,946
1989	-	3	16	38	436	2,081	94	2,255	11,494	176	4,098	21,011
1990	1	2	25	31	384	2,024	86	1,994	11,055	154	3,571	20,372
Outer London												
1981-85[3]	N/A	N/A	N/A	N/A	N/A	N/A	N/A	N/A	N/A	309	4,204	24,327
1989	4	51	294	64	649	3,133	119	1,843	10,183	264	4,461	23,743
1990	4	46	313	59	607	3,125	105	1,965	9,836	239	4,569	23,463
South West Region												
1981-85	17	127	344	62	585	1,586	197	2,475	7,390	440	6,697	19,847
1989	15	110	382	71	428	1,487	189	1,819	7,137	454	4,781	18,877
1990	14	102	425	61	411	1,479	186	1,667	6,852	429	4,496	18,538
Avon												
1981-85	8	50	124	3	29	61	41	450	1,415	86	1,149	3,596
1989	4	31	123	3	24	41	30	312	1,211	74	769	3,087
1990	5	40	154	4	21	70	35	291	1,164	67	710	2,941
Cornwall[1]												
1981-85	-	-	-	10	92	249	14	236	667	39	696	1,984
1989	-	-	-	14	77	289	18	200	769	49	529	2,096
1990	-	-	-	14	78	286	25	161	688	59	501	2,111
Devon												
1981-85	2	10	27	13	131	345	35	570	1,563	82	1,568	4,354
1989	1	12	37	16	108	345	34	386	1,397	80	1,165	4,232
1990	1	13	45	5	94	342	26	339	1,311	65	1,117	4,232
Dorset[1]												
1981-85	-	-	-	4	45	148	23	311	1,112	48	803	2,779
1989	-	-	-	8	30	109	33	261	1,181	77	649	2,731
1990	-	-	-	5	41	154	19	204	1,117	51	548	2,693
Gloucestershire												
1981-85	1	21	54	13	145	369	24	282	705	59	967	2,479
1989	2	15	60	12	84	352	21	192	773	62	547	2,322
1990	5	17	73	18	83	306	18	177	736	75	506	2,169

[1] This county contains no motorways.
[2] Fatal/serious accident data for 1981-85 for London have not been adjusted for the reporting changes in severity in 1984. See note on page 5.
[3] Trunk road data are not available for these years.

Number

	Motorways			Trunk A roads			Principal A roads			All Roads		
	Fatal	Fatal or serious	All severities	Fatal	Fatal or serious	All severities	Fatal	Fatal or serious	All severities	Fatal	Fatal or serious	All severities
Somerset												
1981-85	3	17	43	6	48	117	29	295	789	57	666	1,783
1989	3	18	54	7	28	94	30	225	852	60	482	1,786
1990	1	9	49	2	33	89	31	226	858	46	463	1,871
Wiltshire												
1981-85	4	28	96	12	94	297	32	331	1,138	68	847	2,871
1989	5	34	108	11	77	257	23	243	954	52	640	2,623
1990	2	23	104	13	61	232	32	269	978	66	651	2,521
West Midlands Region												
1981-85	19	138	476	81	639	1,827	190	2,263	7,415	484	6,527	21,030
1989	16	129	656	84	568	2,137	182	1,798	7,653	457	5,208	21,907
1990	23	141	726	57	521	2,014	173	1,755	7,829	437	5,141	22,565
Hereford and Worcester												
1981-85	4	29	104	10	83	245	31	329	1,060	71	859	2,762
1989	2	12	106	21	90	324	32	229	1,039	78	658	2,928
1990	6	36	149	10	83	340	32	224	1,054	71	676	3,045
Shropshire												
1981-85	-	2	4	14	147	363	17	170	473	51	653	1,611
1989	1	5	16	17	133	409	9	154	474	47	594	1,866
1990	-	1	10	17	145	422	19	123	470	56	536	1,865
Staffordshire												
1981-85	8	36	146	25	163	602	36	405	1,577	105	1,209	4,813
1989	5	20	181	14	112	664	52	316	1,780	90	835	5,077
1990	3	24	193	16	103	635	36	315	1,913	93	863	5,417
Warwickshire												
1981-85	4	29	68	19	148	336	23	220	553	77	850	2,078
1989	5	34	98	20	142	440	17	177	624	75	740	2,525
1990	6	43	162	6	132	386	9	175	644	49	748	2,613
West Midlands												
1981-85	4	41	154	12	98	280	84	1,140	3,752	180	2,956	9,767
1989	3	58	255	12	91	300	72	922	3,736	167	2,381	9,511
1990	8	37	212	8	58	231	77	918	3,748	168	2,318	9,625
North West Region												
1981-85	34	180	811	61	441	1,607	248	2,403	11,227	558	6,179	28,643
1989	44	190	1,179	54	421	1,947	231	2,081	12,661	539	5,290	31,794
1990	33	211	1,241	75	432	1,937	228	2,100	12,829	527	5,418	32,494
Cheshire												
1981-85	8	44	198	17	92	400	32	277	1,436	83	778	3,913
1989	15	70	373	10	84	463	35	300	1,587	92	786	4,444
1990	10	59	317	24	106	456	30	275	1,568	87	766	4,257
Cumbria												
1981-85	5	22	62	13	127	355	16	195	605	55	675	2,043
1989	7	27	84	21	122	417	7	163	600	55	555	2,040
1990	3	24	83	29	145	430	21	181	644	69	600	2,124
Greater Manchester												
1981-85	10	59	337	6	50	214	90	971	4,966	178	2,149	11,127
1989	9	42	408	5	55	317	99	841	5,755	183	1,827	12,833
1990	5	51	490	4	43	281	92	854	5,778	170	1,873	13,191
Lancashire												
1981-85	8	40	147	17	113	377	60	554	2,161	135	1,478	5,803
1989	9	38	197	12	91	405	54	426	2,232	116	1,162	5,971
1990	13	60	229	13	88	412	47	409	2,257	126	1,187	6,117
Merseyside												
1981-85	3	14	67	7	59	260	50	406	2,059	107	1,099	5,756
1989	4	13	117	6	69	345	36	351	2,487	93	960	6,506
1990	2	17	122	5	50	358	38	381	2,582	75	992	6,805

14 Accidents: by road class, severity, region[1] and county: 1981-85 average, 1989, 1990 (cont.)

	Motorways			Trunk A roads			Principal A roads			All roads		
	Fatal	Fatal or serious	All severities	Fatal	Fatal or serious	All severities	Fatal	Fatal or serious	All severities	Fatal	Fatal or serious	All severities
England												
1981-85	156	1,059	3,860	654	5,220	16,880	1,859	22,035	87,572	4,333	57,347	218,137
1989	177	1,200	5,892	770	5,432	21,561	1,683	18,460	87,147	4,198	49,328	228,384
1990	167	1,221	6,153	689	5,057	20,743	1,642	17,723	85,917	4,030	47,527	226,441
Wales												
1981-85	5	38	124	62	620	1,746	86	984	3,427	233	3,082	10,583
1989	4	35	166	55	425	1,631	81	859	4,020	214	2,559	11,804
1990	6	42	215	53	445	1,675	97	795	3,889	228	2,435	11,826
Scotland												
1981-85	16	110	265	138	1,010	2,433	228	2,751	7,438	581	7,412	20,471
1989	12	100	349	144	940	2,516	195	2,286	7,299	495	6,289	20,571
1990[2]	10	84	319	127	867	2,527	185	1,937	6,901	490	5,730	20,174
Great Britain												
1981-85	177	1,207	4,249	854	6,850	21,058	2,173	25,769	98,436	5,147	67,842	249,192
1989	193	1,335	6,407	969	6,797	25,708	1,959	21,605	98,466	4,907	58,176	260,759
1990[2]	183	1,347	6,687	869	6,369	24,945	1,924	20,455	96,707	4,748	55,692	258,441

[1] Accident data are not available in this breakdown for Northern Ireland.
[2] 19 accidents in Scotland, originally recorded as motorway accidents, have been re-allocated as A road accidents.

15 Accidents and casualties by severity: vehicles involved by vehicle type: road length: all by selected individual motorways[1] : 1990

	Accidents			Casualties			Vehicles involved				Kilometres open at May 1990[3]
	Fatal	Serious	All severities	Fatal	Serious	All severities	Two-wheel motor vehicles	Cars and LGV	HGV	All vehicles[2]	
England											
M1, M10	27	170	1,025	34	248	1,680	65	2,018	383	2,502	306
M45	-	1	3	-	1	4	-	4	1	5	13
M2	1	12	70	1	15	125	4	104	30	140	42
M3	5	53	206	5	81	335	17	371	44	440	85
M4	16	137	675	18	187	1,105	54	1,270	130	1,474	188
M5	19	64	371	21	111	642	20	637	103	769	262
M6	32	156	932	43	253	1,654	45	1,773	409	2,276	371
M11	3	17	134	3	22	216	8	173	42	228	84
M18	1	10	34	1	12	51	1	48	15	65	46
M20	2	12	64	2	15	110	7	95	16	121	61
M23	5	19	97	8	31	185	6	171	11	189	28
M25	19	136	813	25	182	1,243	53	1,537	275	1,892	188
M26	2	4	15	3	6	19	-	19	4	25	16
M27, M271, M275	4	23	130	5	34	184	13	232	30	277	57
M40	-	15	100	-	19	138	1	174	27	204	48
M42	2	16	74	7	20	112	1	127	30	163	67
M50	-	4	17	-	10	56	-	14	8	23	35
M53	-	7	43	-	7	62	3	73	5	82	33
M54	-	-	18	-	-	22	1	28	4	34	36
M55	-	8	28	-	9	59	5	34	1	41	20
M56	4	11	101	4	18	158	5	176	20	203	58
M57	-	4	32	-	4	53	-	47	4	52	18
M58	-	2	19	-	2	36	-	27	6	33	19
M61	2	5	73	2	7	104	3	128	25	157	38
M62	5	70	398	8	91	616	8	748	142	904	173
M63	2	6	84	2	8	120	3	172	18	197	24
M65	1	4	18	1	7	27	2	30	3	35	23
M66	1	2	36	1	3	57	1	66	8	75	19
M69	-	10	23	-	13	30	-	25	7	32	25
M180 & M181	-	7	19	-	8	30	-	18	7	25	45
Other motorways	2	15	123	2	16	161	14	208	19	252	58
Motorways	155	1,000	5,775	196	1,440	9,394	340	10,547	1,827	12,915	2,529
A(M) roads	12	54	378	15	60	572	26	668	70	778	163
Total (inc A(M) roads)	167	1,054	6,153	211	1,500	9,966	366	11,215	1,897	13,693	2,692
Wales											
Motorways	6	36	213	7	53	347	12	349	56	423	116
A(M) roads	-	-	2	-	-	2	-	4	-	4	4
Total (inc A(M) roads)	6	36	215	7	53	349	12	353	56	427	120
Scotland[4]											
Motorways	10	73	309	11	89	513	6	561	63	647	256
A(M) roads	-	1	10	-	1	13	-	17	-	18	2
Total (inc A(M) roads)	10	74	319	11	90	526	6	578	63	665	258
Great Britain[4]											
Motorways	171	1,109	6,297	214	1,582	10,254	358	11,457	1,946	13,985	2,902
A(M) roads	12	55	390	15	61	587	26	689	70	800	168
Total (inc A(M) roads)	183	1,164	6,687	229	1,643	10,841	384	12,146	2,016	14,785	3,070

[1] Motorway accident data are not available in this breakdown for Northern Ireland.
[2] Includes pedal cycles, buses and coaches and other vehicles.
[3] Excluding slip roads. Data for England from DTp Highways Computing Division.
Data for Wales from Welsh Office and for Scotland from Scottish Office.
[4] 19 accidents in Scotland, originally recorded as motorway accidents, have been re-allocated as A road accidents. There were 28 casualties in these accidents.

37

16 Distribution of accidents by road class and region[1] : 1989 and 1990

percentage (row sums = 100)

	Motorways		Trunk roads		Principal roads		Other roads	
	1989	1990	1989	1990	1989	1990	1989	1990
Northern	1.3	1.1	6.7	6.5	36	37	56	56
Yorkshire & Humberside	1.8	2.1	7.8	8.0	35	34	55	56
East Midlands	2.4	2.6	14.4	14.0	34	33	50	50
Eastern	4.0	4.1	10.8	10.5	31	30	55	55
South Eastern	3.8	3.9	8.3	7.4	36	38	51	51
London	0.7	0.8	11.7	11.7	48	48	39	40
South West	2.0	2.3	7.9	8.0	38	37	52	53
West Midlands	3.0	3.2	9.8	8.9	35	35	52	53
North West	3.7	3.8	6.1	6.0	40	39	50	51
England	2.6	2.7	9.4	9.2	38	38	50	50
Wales	1.4	1.8	13.8	14.2	34	33	51	51
Scotland[2]	1.7	1.6	12.2	12.5	35	34	51	52
Great Britain[2]	2.5	2.6	9.9	9.7	38	37	50	50

[1] Accident data in this breakdown are not available for Northern Ireland.
[2] 19 accidents in Scotland, originally recorded as motorway accidents, have been re-allocated as A road accidents.

17 Motor vehicles, population, area and road length (motorways and built-up and non built-up roads: by trunk and principal): by region: 1990

Thousands/number

	Motor vehicles currently licensed[1] (thousands)	Population mid year (home) (thousands)	Area in hectares (thousands)	Road length (kilometres)				
				Motorways[2]	Built-up[3]		Non built-up[3]	
					Trunk	Principal	Trunk	Principal
Northern	872	2,583.3	859	56	19	512	414	830
Yorkshire and Humberside	1,995	4,951.9	1,542	320	120	1,145	639	1,392
East Midlands	1,758	4,018.7	1,563	184	168	777	1,068	1,889
Eastern	3,014	5,758.1	2,100	316	108	1,078	1,191	2,207
South East	3,481	6,964.4	1,722	492	122	1,529	907	2,264
London	2,831	6,794.4	158	57	209	1,324	117	39
South West	2,403	4,666.5	2,385	304	85	1,210	1,218	2,815
West Midlands	2,456	5,219.3	1,301	405	142	1,115	803	1,571
North West	2,798	6,880.7	1,414	558	125	1,681	731	1,478
England[4]	21,640	47,837.3	13,044	2,692	1,097	10,371	7,087	14,485
Wales	1,222	2,881.4	2,077	120	212	837	1,367	1,788
Scotland	1,811	5,102.4	7,717	258	223	1,250	2,688	6,418
Great Britain[4]	24,673	55,821.1	22,838	3,070	1,532	12,462	11,087	22,572
Northern Ireland[5]	543	1,589.4	1,412	112	487		1,726	
United Kingdom[4] [5]	25,216	57,410.5	24,250	3,182	14,577		35,385	

[1] Includes agricultural tractors, combine harvesters, mowing machines, digging machines, mobile cranes, works trucks, pedestrian controlled vehicles, tricycles, showmen's vehicles, general haulage tractors, public service vehicles and exempt vehicles, which represent 2.8 per cent of the total.
[2] Excluding slip roads. Data for England from DTp Highways Computing Division. Total for England includes figures for non-trunk motorways not included in regional totals. Data for Wales from Welsh Office and Scotland from Scottish Office.
[3] As at April 1990. Taken from DTp Transport Statistics Report 'Road lengths in Great Britain 1990'.
[4] Including region of registration unknown.
[5] Trunk and Principal road length data are not available for Northern Ireland. Data are for all A roads.

18 Motor traffic distribution between regions[1] : by motorway and built-up and non built-up trunk and principal roads: 1988-1990 average

per cent

	Motorways	Built-up		Non built-up		All major
		Trunk	Principal	Trunk	Principal	roads
Northern	1%	1%	4%	5%	5%	4%
Yorkshire & Humberside	8%	7%	9%	7%	7%	8%
East Midlands	6%	9%	6%	10%	9%	7%
Eastern	16%	7%	8%	17%	14%	13%
South East	19%	9%	14%	15%	19%	16%
London	2%	31%	15%	4%	0%	7%
South West	9%	7%	9%	10%	14%	10%
West Midlands	14%	9%	10%	7%	8%	10%
North West	17%	7%	15%	6%	8%	12%
England	92%	86%	89%	82%	84%	87%
Wales	3%	7%	4%	6%	5%	5%
Scotland	5%	8%	7%	12%	11%	9%
Great Britain	100%	100%	100%	100%	100%	100%

[1] Traffic data are not available for Northern Ireland.

19 Motor traffic distribution between motorways, built-up and non built-up trunk and principal roads: by region[1] : 1988-1990 average

per cent

	Motorways	Built-up		Non built-up		All major
		Trunk	Principal	Trunk	Principal	roads
Northern	8%	1%	28%	31%	31%	100%
Yorkshire & Humberside	25%	4%	31%	21%	19%	100%
East Midlands	19%	5%	21%	30%	26%	100%
Eastern	28%	2%	17%	29%	23%	100%
South East	28%	2%	23%	21%	25%	100%
London	7%	18%	60%	13%	1%	100%
South West	21%	3%	23%	23%	30%	100%
West Midlands	34%	4%	28%	17%	17%	100%
North West	35%	3%	34%	12%	15%	100%
England	25%	4%	28%	22%	21%	100%
Wales	14%	6%	24%	31%	25%	100%
Scotland	15%	4%	23%	31%	27%	100%
Great Britain	24%	4%	27%	23%	22%	100%

[1] Traffic data are not available for Northern Ireland.

DEFINITIONS

Accident: Accidents involving personal injury occuring on the public highway (including footways) in which a road vehicle is involved and which becomes known to the police within 30 days of its occurance. The vehicle need not be moving and it need not be involved in a collision. One accident may give rise to several *casualties*. Damage-only accidents are not included in this publication.

'A' Roads: All purpose *trunk* roads and *principal* local authority roads.

Adults: Persons aged 15 years and over (except where otherwise stated).

Built-up Roads: Roads with speed limits (ignoring temporary limits) of 40 mph or less. The pre-1982 definition of 'built-up areas' referred to the same roads but the general nature of the area was never relevant. 'Non built-up roads' refer to speed limits over 40 mph. *Motorways* are included with non built-up roads unless otherwise stated. In tables where data for *motorways* are shown separately, the totals for built-up and non built-up roads exclude *motorway accidents*. In comparing such tables with those involving a built-up/non built-up split only, negligible error will be made by assuming that *motorway accidents* were all on non built-up roads.

Casualty: A person *killed* or injured in an *accident*. Casualties are classified as either *killed*, *seriously injured* or *slightly injured*.

Darkness/Night-time: From half-an-hour after sunset until half-an-hour before sunrise, ie 'lighting-up time'.

Fatal Accident: An *accident* in which at least one person is *killed* (but excluding confirmed suicides).

Heavy Goods Vehicles (HGVs): Goods vehicles over 1.5 tons (1.524 tonnes) unladen weight.

Killed: Human *casualties* who sustained injuries resulting in death within 30 days of the *accident*.

Light Goods Vehicles (LGVs): Goods vehicles of less than 1.5 tons (1.524 tonnes) unladen weight.

Licensed Vehicles: The stock of vehicles currently licensed on 31 December, when the annual census is taken at the Driver and Vehicle Licensing Centre (DVLC).

London: Where possible, data for London have been split into Inner and Outer London. Inner London comprises the City of London and the boroughs of Westminster, Camden, Islington, Hackney, Tower Hamlets, Lewisham, Southwark, Lambeth, Wandsworth, Hammersmith, Kensington and Chelsea, Newham, and Haringey. Outer London is all other London boroughs, and includes Heathrow Airport. See also *Regions*.

Main Roads: These are *motorways*, A(M) and *A class roads* (both *trunk* and *principal*).

Motorways: Data given for motorways are for both motorways and A(M) roads except where otherwise noted. The motorway lengths given in Tables 16 and 17 are main line lengths and exclude associated slip roads.

Motorway Accident: Accidents on *motorways* include those on associated slip roads and those at junctions between *motorways* and other roads where the *accident* cannot be clearly allocated to the other road.

Other Roads: These are 'B' and 'C' class roads and unclassified roads, including 'road class not reported'.

Pedestrians: In addition to those walking on footways, also included are persons riding toy cycles on the footway, persons pushing bicycles or pushing or pulling other vehicles or operating pedestrian controlled vehicles, those leading or herding animals, occupants of prams and wheelchairs, and those who alight safely from vehicles.

Population: The population data used in calculating rates are the Registrar General's estimate of the resident population at 30 June, 1990. The estimates include residents who are temporarily outside the country, and exclude both foreign visitors and members of HM armed forces who are stationed abroad.

Principal Roads: Roads for which County Councils (Regional and Island Authorities in Scotland) are the Highway Authority. The classified *principal roads* (which include local authority *motorways*) are those of regional and urban strategic importance.

Regions: In tables where data are disaggregated by region, Department of Transport regions are used, as illustrated by the map on page 6. Greater London is not strictly a region and special arrangements apply, in that the responsibility falls to the London Regional Office (LRO) in DTp headquarters. The South East and Eastern regions do not include any of the Greater London area.

Serious Accident: An *accident* in which at least one person is *seriously injured* but no one is *killed* (other than a confirmed suicide).

Serious Injury: An injury for which a person is detained in hospital as an 'in-patient', or any of the following injuries whether or not the *casualty* was detained in hospital: fractures, concussion, internal injuries, crushings, severe cuts and lacerations, severe general shock requiring medical treatment, and injuries causing death 30 or more days after the *accident*. An injured *casualty* is coded as seriously or *slightly injured* by the police on the basis of information available within a short time of the *accident*. This generally will not include the result of a medical examination, but may include the fact of being detained in hospital, the reasons for which may vary from area to area.

Severity: The severity of an *accident* is the severity of the most severely injured *casualty*.

Slight Accident: An *accident* in which at least one person is *slightly injured*, but no one is *killed* or *seriously injured*.

Slight Injury: An injury of a minor character such as a sprain, bruise or cut which are not judged to be severe, or slight shock requiring roadside attention only.

Trunk Roads: Roads comprising the national network of through routes for which the Secretary of State for Transport in England and the Secretaries of State for Scotland and Wales are the highway authorities. The network contains both *motorways*, which legally are special roads reserved for certain classes of traffic, and all-purpose roads which are open to all classes of traffic.

Accident Record Attendant Circumstances

1.1 Record Type
1 New accident record
5 Amended accident record
[1] (1 2)

1.2 Police Force
[ ] (3 4)

1.3 Accident Ref No
[ ] (5 6 7 8 9 10 11)

1.4 Severity of Accident
1 Fatal   2 Serious   3 Slight
[ ] (12)

1.5 Number of Vehicles
[ ] (13 14 15)

1.6 Number of Casualty Records
[ ] (16 17 18)

1.7 Date
Day (19 20)   Month (21 22)   Year (23 24)
[ ] [ ] [ ]

1.8 Day of Week
1 Sunday   2 Monday
3 Tuesday   4 Wednesday
5 Thursday   6 Friday
7 Saturday
[ ] (25)

1.9 Time
Hrs (26 27)   Mins (28 29)
24 hour
[ ] [ ]

1.10 Local Authority
[ ] (30 31 32)

1.11 Location
10 digit reference No
Easting (33 34 35 36 37)
Northing (38 39 40 41 42)

1.12 1st Road Class
1 Motorway
2 A (M)
3 A
4 B
5 C
6 Unclassified
7 Local }
8 Authority } Use Only
9 }
[ ] (43)

1.13 1st Road Number
[ ] (44 45 46 47)

1.14 Carriageway Type or Markings
1 Roundabout (on circular highway)
2 One way street
3 Dual carriageway - 2 lanes
4 Dual carriageway - 3 or more lanes
5 Single carriageway - single track road
6 Single carriageway - 2 lanes (one each direction)
7 Single carriageway - 3 lanes (two way capacity)
8 Single carriageway - 4 or more lanes (two way capacity)
9 Unknown
[ ] (48)

1.15 Speed Limit
mph
[0] (49 50 51)

1.16 Junction Detail
0 Not at or within 20 metres of junction
1 Roundabout
2 Mini-roundabout
3 'T' or staggered junction
4 'Y' junction
5 Slip road
6 Crossroads
7 Multiple junction
8 Using private drive or entrance
9 Other junction
[0] (52 53)

--- Junction Accidents Only ---

1.17 Junction Control
1 Authorised person
2 Automatic traffic signal
3 Stop sign
4 Give way sign or markings
5 Uncontrolled
[ ] (54)

1.18 2nd Road Class
1 Motorway
2 A (M)
3 A
4 B
5 C
6 Unclassified
7 Local }
8 Authority } Use Only
9 }
[ ] (55)

1.19 2nd Road Number
[ ] (56 57 58 59)

1.20 Pedestrian Crossing Facilities
0 No crossing facilities within 50 metres
1 Zebra
2 Zebra crossing controlled by school crossing patrol
3 Zebra crossing controlled by other authorised person
4 Pelican
5 Other light controlled crossing
6 Other sites controlled by school crossing patrol
7 Other sites controlled by other authorised person
8 Central refuge - no other controls
9 Footbridge or subway
[0] (60 61)

1.21 Light Conditions
DAYLIGHT
1 Street lights 7 metres or more high
2 Street lights under 7 metres high
3 No street lighting
4 Daylight street lighting unknown
DARKNESS
5 Street lights 7 metres or more high (lit)
6 Street lights under 7 metres high (lit)
7 No street lighting
8 Street lights unlit
9 Darkness street lighting unknown
[ ] (62)

1.22 Weather
1 Fine (without high winds)
2 Raining (without high winds)
3 Snowing (without high winds)
4 Fine with high winds
5 Raining with high winds
6 Snowing with high winds
7 Fog (or mist if hazard)
8 Other
9 Unknown
[ ] (63)

1.23 Road Surface Condition
1 Dry
2 Wet/Damp
3 Snow
4 Frost/Ice
5 Flood (surface water over 3cms (1 inch) deep)
[ ] (64)

1.24 Special Conditions at Site
0 None
1 Automatic Traffic Signal-out
2 Automatic Traffic Signal partially defective
3 Permanent road signing defective or obscured
4 Road works present
5 Road surface defective
[ ] (65)

1.25 Carriageway Hazards
0 None
1 Dislodged vehicle load in carriageway
2 Other object in carriageway
3 Involvement with previous accident
4 Dog in carriageway
5 Other animal in carriageway
[ ] (66)

1.26 Overtaking Manoeuvre Patterns
No longer required by the Department of Transport
[ ] (67)

1.27 DTp Special Projects
[ ] (68 69 70 71)

Vehicle Record

2.1 Record Type
1 2
[ ][2]

1 New vehicle record
5 Amended vehicle record

2.2 Police Force
3 4
[ ][ ]

2.3 Accident Ref No
5 6 7 8 9 10 11
[ ][ ][ ][ ][ ][ ][ ]

2.4 Vehicle Ref No
12 13 14
[ ][ ][ ]

2.5 Type of Vehicle
15 16
[ ][ ]

01 Pedal cycle
02 Moped
03 Motor scooter
04 Motor cycle
05 Combination
06 Invalid Tricycle
07 Other three-wheeled car
08 Taxi
09 Car (four wheeled)
10 Minibus/Motor caravan
11 PSV
12 Goods not over 1 1/2 tons UW (1.52 tonnes)
13 Goods over 1 1/2 tons UW (1.52 tonnes)
14 Other motor vehicle
15 Other non motor vehicle

2.6 Towing and Articulation
17
[ ]

0 No tow/articulation
1 Articulated vehicle
2 Double/multiple trailer
3 Caravan
4 Single trailer
5 Other tow

2.7 Manoeuvres
18 19
[ ][ ]

01 Reversing
02 Parked
03 Waiting to go ahead but held up
04 Stopping
05 Starting
06 U turn
07 Turning left
08 Waiting to turn left
09 Turning right
10 Waiting to turn right
11 Changing lane to left
12 Changing lane to right
13 Overtaking moving vehicle on its offside
14 Overtaking stationary vehicle on its offside
15 Overtaking on nearside
16 Going ahead left hand bend
17 Going ahead right hand bend
18 Going ahead other

2.8 Vehicle Movement Compass Point
20 21
[ ][ ]
From To

1 N   2 NE   3 E
4 SE   5 S   6 SW
7 W   8 NW

or [0][0] Parked - not at kerb

[0] Parked - at kerb

2.9 Vehicle Location at time of Accident
22 23
[ ][ ]

01 Leaving the main road
02 Entering the main road
03 On main road
04 On minor road
05 On service road
06 On lay-by or hard shoulder
07 Entering lay-by or hard shoulder
08 Leaving lay-by or hard shoulder
09 On a cycleway
10 Not on carriageway

2.10 Junction Location of Vehicle at First Impact
24
[ ]

0 Not at junction (or within 20 metres/22 yards)
1 Vehicle approaching junction/vehicle parked at junction approach
2 Vehicle in middle of junction
3 Vehicle cleared junction/vehicle parked at junction exit
4 Did not impact

2.11 Skidding and Overturning
25
[ ]

0 No skidding, jackknifing or overturning
1 Skidded
2 Skidded and overturned
3 Jackknifed
4 Jackknifed and overturned
5 Overturned

2.12 Hit Object In Carriageway
26 27
[ ][ ]

00 None
01 Previous accident
02 Road works
03 Parked vehicle - lit
04 Parked vehicle - unlit
05 Bridge (roof)
06 Bridge (side)
07 Bollard/refuge
08 Open door of vehicle
09 Central island or roundabout
10 Kerb
11 Other object

2.13 Vehicle Leaving Carriageway
28
[ ]

0 Did not leave carriageway
1 Left carriageway nearside
2 Left carriageway nearside and rebounded
3 Left carriageway straight ahead at junction
4 Left carriageway offside onto central reservation
5 Left carriageway offside onto central reservation and rebounded
6 Left carriageway offside crossed central reservation
7 Left carriageway offside
8 Left carriageway offside and rebounded

2.14 Hit Object Off Carriageway
29 30
[ ][ ]

00 None
01 Road sign/Traffic signal
02 Lamp post
03 Telegraph pole/Electricity pole
04 Tree
05 Bus stop/Bus shelter
06 Central crash barrier
07 Nearside or offside crash barrier
08 Submerged in water (completely)
09 Entered ditch
10 Other permanent object

2.15 Vehicle Prefix/Suffix Letter
31
[ ]

Prefix/Suffix letter or one of the following codes -
0 More than twenty years old (at end of year)
1 Unknown/cherished number/not applicable
2 Foreign/diplomatic
3 Military
4 Trade plates

2.16 First Point of Impact
32
[ ]

0 Did not impact
1 Front
2 Back
3 Offside
4 Nearside

2.17 Other Vehicle Hit (VEH Ref No)
33 34 35
[ ][ ][ ]

2.18 Part(s) Damaged
36 37 38
[ ][ ][ ]

0 None
1 Front
2 Back
3 Offside
4 Nearside
5 Roof
6 Underside
7 all four sides

2.19 No of Axles
39
[ ]

No longer required by the Department of Transport

2.20 Maximum Permissible Gross Weight
40 41
[ ][ ]

Metric tonnes (Goods vehicle only)

2.21 Sex of Driver
42
[ ]

1 Male
2 Female
3 Not traced

2.22 Age of Driver
43 44
[ ][ ]

(Years estimated if necessary)

2.23 Breath Test
45
[ ]

0 Not applicable
1 Positive
2 Negative
3 Not requested
4 Failed to provide
5 Driver not contacted at time

2.24 Hit and Run
46
[ ]

0 Other
1 'Hit and run'
2 Non-stop vehicle not hit

2.25 DTp Special Projects
47 48 49 50
[ ][ ][ ][ ]

43

Casualty Record

3.1 Record Type
|1|2|
|3| |

1 New casualty record
5 Amended casualty record

3.2 Police Force
3 4

3.3 Accident Ref No
5 6 7 8 9 10 11

3.4 Vehicle Ref No
12 13 14

3.5 Casualty Ref No
15 16 17

3.6 Casualty Class
18

1 Driver or Rider
2 Vehicle or pillion passenger
3 Pedestrian

3.7 Sex of Casualty
19

1 Male
2 Female

3.8 Age of Casualty
20 21

(Years estimated if necessary)

3.9 Severity of Casualty
22

1 Fatal
2 Serious
3 Slight

3.10 Pedestrian Location
23 24

00 Not pedestrian
01 In carriageway crossing on pedestrian crossing
02 In carriageway crossing within zig-zag lines approach to the crossing
03 In carriageway crossing within zig-zag lines exit the crossing
04 In carriageway crossing elsewhere within 50 metres of pedestrian crossing
05 In carriageway crossing elsewhere
06 On footway or verge
07 On refuge or central island or reservation
08 In centre of carriageway not on refuge or central island
09 In carriageway not crossing
10 Unknown

3.11 Pedestrian Movement
25

0 Not pedestrian
1 Crossing from drivers nearside
2 Crossing from drivers nearside - masked by parked or stationary vehicle
3 Crossing from drivers offside
4 Crossing from drivers offside - masked by parked or stationary vehicle
5 In carriageway stationary - not crossing (standing or playing)
6 In carriageway stationary - not crossing (standing or playing) - masked by parked or stationary vehicle
7 Walking along in carriageway facing traffic
8 Walking along in carriageway back to traffic
9 Unknown

3.12 Pedestrian Direction
26

Compass point bound
1 N
2 NE
3 E
4 SE
5 S
6 SW
7 W
8 NW
or 0 - Pedestrian - standing still

3.13 School Pupil Casualty
27

0 Not a school pupil
1 Pupil on journey to/from school
2 Pupil NOT on journey to/from school

3.14 Seat Belt Usage
28

0 Not car or van
1 Safety belt in use
2 Safety belt fitted - not in use
3 Safety belt not fitted
4 Child safety belt/harness fitted - in use
5 Child safety belt/harness fitted - not in use
6 Child safety belt/harness not fitted
7 Unknown

3.15 Car Passenger
29

0 Not a car passenger
1 Front seat car passenger
2 Rear seat car passenger

3.16 PSV Passenger
30

0 Not a PSV passenger
1 Boarding
2 Alighting
3 Standing passenger
4 Seated passenger

3.17 DTp Special Projects
31 32 33 34